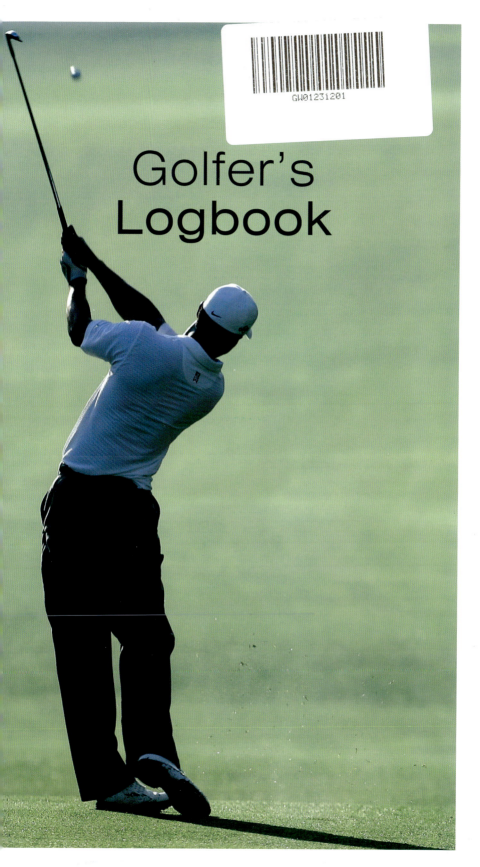

Golfer's
Logbook

GOLFER'S LOGBOOK.

Published by A&C Black Publishers Ltd
38 Soho Square, London W1D 3HB
www.acblack.com

Conceived, edited and designed by
Marshall Editions
The Old Brewery
6 Blundell Street
London N7 9BH
www.quarto.com

ISBN: 978-0-7136-8940-2

Originated in Hong Kong by Modern Age
Printed in China by Midas Printing International Ltd

Publisher: Richard Green
Commissioning editor: Paul Docherty
Senior designer: Sarah Robson
Project editor: Deborah Hercun
Editorial and design: Hart McLeod
Production: Nikki Ingram

10 9 8 7 6 5 4 3 2 1

Cover photo: ©Aldo Torelli/Staff/Getty Images

Golfer's
Logbook

Lee Pearce

Contents

Using your logbook
Improving your game

Michelle Wie looks at a yardage chart; professionals take careful note of every aspect of the game.

It may be rare (and certainly not recommended by publicists) to start out by telling what the book is not. But this book is *not* a complete guide to golf. That said, it will almost certainly save you many more shots than a complete guide because this book looks specifically at *your* game.

Your logbook pages

By completing the logbook pages you will build an accurate and detailed picture of your own game, round by round over 50 rounds. By using the analysis pages, after every 10 rounds, you will then be able to use the information gathered to identify trends and problem areas. Are you regularly failing in bunkers? Are you finding the fairway frequently enough? Is your putting letting you down?

Hopefully you will notice positive trends too, particularly as you work on the areas where you feel in need of improvement.

Your real strengths and weaknesses

Once you understand where problems are occurring you can turn to the fault fixer pages (from page 128) to look for remedies. Importantly the logbook analysis will help you recognize your true strengths and weaknesses, not just the ones you thought you had. Golfers frequently grumble about one aspect of their play because they perceive it as a weakness whereas, in fact, they are losing a greater number of shots in other areas. Of course you can work on every part of your game – but it's important to know where most shots can be saved in the short term.

The fault fixer pages vary in content. In many cases you will be taken back to basics. The page will act as a reminder of fundamental skills and good practice. In other cases the pages will take you further, building on what you already have learned from your golf pro or instruction books and DVDs.

All areas include "Pro Tips" where extra tips and hints are included. Many also include "Reminders" that visually refresh your memory of basic issues such as technique, equipment, and practice. In many cases the photographs are a good device for additional instructional points as well as providing us amateur golfers with some aspirational shots!

Completing and customising your logbook

The logbook is usable equally whether you play the same course all the time or visit a number of venues. We recommend that you complete the pages at home or in the clubhouse relatively quickly after a round. You will remember the holes and can accurately record such points as short and long putts, and fairways missed.

You can also add extra notes if you feel they are relevant – make the pages work for you and your game.

PRO TIP Develop and improve your game by working on one thing at a time. Don't try to do too much at once.

Thinking about your game
A fresh approach to go with your logbook

One of the key things that a book like this may do is to help you think afresh about your golf. It is a thinking game. Technique and physical ability will only take you so far; without some thought you will soon reach a brick wall in your improvement.

The bigger picture
Of course, you need to think on every shot – what club, what approach, what game situation. You also need to think about your strategy and course management. These are points that you have probably already considered. The "Fault fixer" pages also tackle these issues. Beyond this, however, are you thinking about the bigger picture, about your approach to the game as a whole? What can you expect to get from the game? What are you prepared to put in? What sort of game do you want to play?

The objective view
The fact that you are planning to record every score over a large number of rounds and analyse the results shows you are already thinking differently from many others in the game. You will know your game so much better as a result. You will be looking at yourself objectively, largely from the outside. Are you also prepared to look at your general game from an outsider's perspective? It is worth measuring your game against new

Think very carefully about how you approach a round. Do you have the right clubs? You can have a maximum of 14 in your bag so you may as well take the extra wedge or wood if you have room. Don't skimp on what you take around if you are using a cart or a large push bag. Water or energy drinks, plus cereal bars, bananas, or other foods can all accompany you. Make sure also that you have (if appropriate) spare gloves, warm clothes, or sun screen.

criteria and not just how you feel about it. You may be disappointed in a score, but how much better is your golf now than a year ago? How much better than three years ago? Your handicap implies that you are expected to par, for example, six holes in a round (and bogey the rest). Are you overly frustrated when you don't hit par on a particular hole? Don't forget, in this context, your handicap isn't something you are expected to hit every time you walk on a course, only when you are playing well.

Not every game needs to be the same. Sometimes you want to go out with a small number of clubs (a "carry-bag" cuts down distances you walk and length of round) focusing on one part of your game. Some competitions are for a set number of clubs – typically six or seven – and scores are rarely worse than when players can use their normal set.

Confidence and realistic goals

The large amount of televised professional golf is also likely to make us set unrealistic goals. We can't all hit perfect draws and magical chips like Phil Mickleson so we shouldn't expect to when we play at the weekend. (The fact is we occasionally hit a special shot and wonder why we can't do it all the time.)

A fresh and realistic view of your game may have one important result. It may give you greater confidence. The fact (probably) is that you are actually improving and doing better than some others in your club. You don't need to stop trying to improve, but you can take strength from what you have achieved before moving forward.

Rules of Golf

In most social play the rules are merely there to help you resolve any tricky issue. A quick check will be all that is needed. However, in competition or more serious games, it is important that you are familiar with the rules and, ideally, you have an abridged set in your golf bag. With knowledge of the rules you can not only confidently answer any challenges or questions, but you can also take advantage of certain situations (such as around hazards, in traps, with staked trees, or on paths) where sometimes relief can be taken.

GOLF RULES IN BRIEF
2004-2007
as approved by R&A Rules Limited

How to use this book
Your logbook pages

You can record all the information as you go round the course, but this may be too distracting. It's probably best to complete the pages as soon as possible after the round. You will readily recall points such as fairways hit and putts short or long. It's good practice to record every round you play, but don't be too hard on yourself if you have a real disaster. You are an amateur,

An important aspect of golf. Weather will affect your shot decisions.

Make a note of your playing handicap each time. It will affect Stableford scores of course.

Be realistic. If you have a bad hole, award yourself a mulligan, or your opponent lets you have a free drop, don't be too harsh on the scorecard.

These are putts on the green – don't count any putts you choose to take from off the green.

Yardages are not the most critical issue, but recording them allows you to build up a picture of your success on shorter or longer holes.

Left, on, or right of fairway.

The "S" is for short of the fairway.

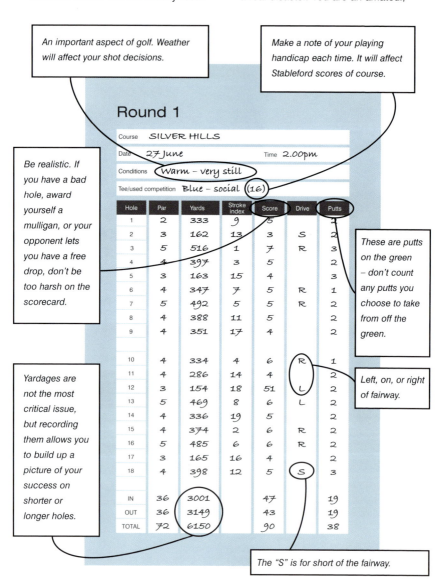

Round 1

Course SILVER HILLS

Date 27 June   Time 2.00pm

Conditions Warm – very still

Tee/used competition Blue – social (16)

Hole	Par	Yards	Stroke index	Score	Drive	Putts
1	2	333	9	5		2
2	3	162	13	3	S	2
3	5	516	1	7	R	3
4	4	397	3	5		2
5	3	163	15	4		3
6	4	347	7	5	R	1
7	5	492	5	5	R	2
8	4	388	11	5		2
9	4	351	17	4		2
10	4	334	4	6	R	1
11	4	286	14	4		2
12	3	154	18	51	L	2
13	5	469	8	6	L	2
14	4	336	19	5		2
15	4	374	2	6	R	2
16	5	485	6	6	R	2
17	3	165	16	4		2
18	4	398	12	5	S	3
IN	36	3001		47		19
OUT	36	3149		43		19
TOTAL	72	6150		90		38

playing the game for fun. Tear up the card and record the next round. Over 50 rounds you will learn a lot about your game; missing a few rounds out won't hurt. Remember too that the pages are for you. You can customize them to include what you want, such as driver used, hybrid shots from fairway, or type of ball. Add anything to build up a complete picture.

This won't always be a huge drive or amazing approach shot. Sometimes a rescue from the rough or a pressure putt might qualify.

This means reaching the green in one shot on the par 3s, two shots on the par 4s, and three on the par 5s.

This may mean just onto the fairway (from a difficult lie), or within 20 feet if you have a simpler shot.

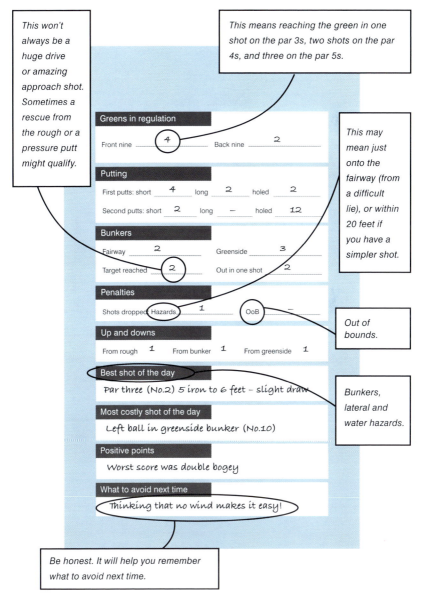

Greens in regulation

Front nine _____ 4 _____ Back nine _____ 2 _____

Putting

First putts: short _____ 4 _____ long _____ 2 _____ holed _____ 2 _____

Second putts: short _____ 2 _____ long _____ — _____ holed _____ 12 _____

Bunkers

Fairway _____ 2 _____ Greenside _____ 3 _____

Target reached _____ 2 _____ Out in one shot _____ 2 _____

Penalties

Shots dropped Hazards _____ 1 _____ OoB _____ — _____

Up and downs

From rough _____ 1 _____ From bunker _____ 1 _____ From greenside _____ 1 _____

Best shot of the day

Par three (No.2) 5 iron to 6 feet – slight draw

Most costly shot of the day

Left ball in greenside bunker (No.10)

Positive points

Worst score was double bogey

What to avoid next time

Thinking that no wind makes it easy!

Out of bounds.

Bunkers, lateral and water hazards.

Be honest. It will help you remember what to avoid next time.

How to use this book
Your analysis pages

It is intended that you complete the pages after every 10 rounds but you can look at any time to note trends and see progress. An analysis after eight rounds will be valuable. You will soon spot where shots can be saved. You can then turn to the fault fixer pages to find ways of putting it right.

The Pro Tip in the introduction is very important, however. Just tackle one thing at a time. It doesn't even need to be the worst aspect of your game to begin with.

You may wish to keep an extra notes of birdies... and even eagles!

While birdies and pars may be the goal, the improving golfer wants to eliminate double bogeys (and worse) as much as possible. Two over par for any hole really damages the card.

This is plus or minus your handicap. Make a note here too if your playing handicap changes during the course of the 10 rounds.

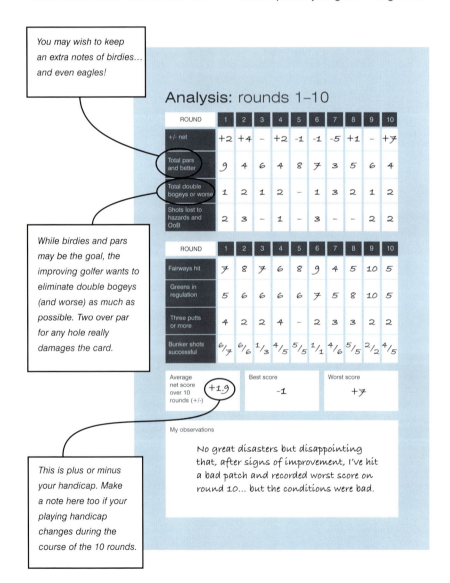

Analysis: rounds 1–10

ROUND	1	2	3	4	5	6	7	8	9	10
+/- net	+2	+4	–	+2	-1	-1	-5	+1	–	+7
Total pars and better	9	4	6	4	8	7	3	5	6	4
Total double bogeys or worse	1	2	1	2	–	1	3	2	1	2
Shots lost to hazards and OoB	2	3	–	1	–	3	–	–	2	2

ROUND	1	2	3	4	5	6	7	8	9	10
Fairways hit	7	8	7	6	8	9	4	5	10	5
Greens in regulation	5	6	6	6	6	7	5	8	10	5
Three putts or more	4	2	2	4	–	2	3	3	2	2
Bunker shots successful	$6/7$	$6/6$	$1/3$	$4/5$	$5/5$	$1/1$	$4/6$	$5/5$	$2/2$	$4/5$

Average net score over 10 rounds (+/-)	Best score	Worst score
+1.9	-1	+7

My observations

No great disasters but disappointing that, after signs of improvement, I've hit a bad patch and recorded worst score on round 10... but the conditions were bad.

To rectify a poor swing to gain better direction from the tee might take a few practice sessions and a lesson or two. Eliminating short putts, for example, can be a much simpler process and may show immediate rewards.

The Stableford scoring system is the best for comparing scores. "Medal" or strokeplay golf will show up very bad holes (which everybody has from time to time), which can distort averages. In Stableford, on a par 4, a "13" will still only count as zero points.

The birdie scored here was worth four points. If you play on the same course most of the time you could record an eclectic score, your best Stableford tally on each hole. Very soon your eclectic will be over 40 points and rising. An eclectic score is just a reminder of what you could do if you hit every shot perfectly on the same round.

Trends: Stableford analysis

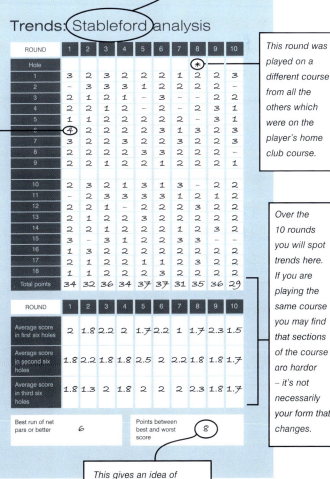

ROUND	1	2	3	4	5	6	7	8	9	10
Hole								⊛		
1	3	2	3	2	2	2	1	2	2	3
2	–	3	3	3	1	2	2	2	2	–
3	2	1	2	1	–	3	–	–	2	2
4	2	2	1	2	–	2	–	2	3	1
5	1	1	2	2	2	2	2	–	3	1
6	④	2	2	2	2	3	1	3	2	3
7	3	2	2	3	2	2	3	2	2	3
8	2	2	2	2	3	3	2	2	2	–
9	2	2	1	2	2	1	2	2	2	1
10	2	3	2	1	3	1	3	–	2	2
11	–	2	3	3	3	3	1	2	1	2
12	2	2	1	–	2	2	2	3	2	2
13	2	1	2	2	3	2	2	2	2	2
14	2	2	1	2	2	2	1	2	3	2
15	3	–	3	1	2	2	3	3	–	–
16	1	3	2	2	2	2	2	2	2	2
17	2	1	2	2	1	1	2	3	2	2
18	1	1	2	2	2	3	2	2	2	2
Total points	34	32	36	34	37	37	31	35	36	29

ROUND	1	2	3	4	5	6	7	8	9	10
Average score in first six holes	2	1.8	2.2	2	1.7	2.2	1	1.7	2.3	1.5
Average score in second six holes	1.8	2.2	1.8	1.8	2.5	2	2.2	1.8	1.8	1.7
Average score in third six holes	1.8	1.3	2	1.8	2	2	2	2.3	1.8	1.7

Best run of net pars or better	6	Points between best and worst score	8

This round was played on a different course from all the others which were on the player's home club course.

Over the 10 rounds you will spot trends here. If you are playing the same course you may find that sections of the course are harder – it's not necessarily your form that changes.

This gives an idea of your consistency.

Planning to play for 18 holes
Hot and cold streaks during your round

Mental approach

The last thing you want to do is over-analyse why you are playing well. Enjoy it and hope your form lasts. Importantly though, you want to be able to retrieve a bad situation. A bad hole or two need not be the end of the world, but sometimes it can lead to it! Your mental approach to golf is vital and, as we all know, you'll tend to remember every bad shot you ever hit but rarely remember the good ones. How many times during the monthly medal do you have a poor front nine, and then relax because the score has gone, and play really well?

Positive thoughts

The first thing is to try to stay focused and positive. If you face a tough shot from the rough or a narrow drive, a tricky chip, or a long curling putt, don't think about what can go wrong. Make your club and shot

choice and then visualize the shot in your head a few times before addressing the ball. The likelihood of playing the shot better is improved immensely. If you have played a similar shot successfully before, then recall that and try to replicate it.

Be patient

Because the mind plays such a big part in golf, if at any stage at address you feel either uncomfortable or think you might have the wrong club, then this gut feeling is normally correct, so step back and reassess. This key piece of advice relates especially to your shots when you're having a bad spell. Don't rush them, don't hit if you are unhappy with anything. Importantly remember that the game is over 18 holes and three-down can be rectified in three holes and one birdie can make a medal score suddenly look a whole lot better.

> **PRO TIP** Visualize every shot, picture the ball going exactly where you want before actually playing the stroke.

A lot can happen in golf over the last holes as tiredness, lack of concentration, and a little bit of pressure all play their part. At the end of the round, howovor, tho handshake reminds everybody that it is just a game, even if a very important one as here where Stewart Cink and team mate JJ Henry (R) of USA shake hands on the 18th green with Paul Casey (L) and Robert Karlsson of Europe after they halved their match during the morning fourballs of the first day of the Ryder Cup in 2006.

Logbook:
Record your shots and analyze your scores

Round 1

Course						
Date				Time		
Conditions						
Tee/used competition						

Hole	Par	Yards	Stroke index	Score	Drive	Putts
1						
2						
3						
4						
5						
6						
7						
8						
9						
10						
11						
12						
13						
14						
15						
16						
17						
18						
IN						
OUT						
TOTAL						

Greens in regulation

Front nine.. Back nine...

Putting

First putts: short.......................... long .... holed....................

Second putts: short .... long .... holed....................

Bunkers

Fairway.. Greenside...

Target reached .... Out in one shot................................

Penalties

Shots dropped: Hazards .... OoB.......................................

Up and downs

From rough .... From bunker .... From greenside..............

Best shot of the day

....

Most costly shot of the day

....

Positive points

....

What to avoid next time

....

Round 2

Course

Date   **Time**

Conditions

Tee/used competition

Hole	Par	Yards	Stroke index	Score	Drive	Putts
1						
2						
3						
4						
5						
6						
7						
8						
9						
10						
11						
12						
13						
14						
15						
16						
17						
18						
IN						
OUT						
TOTAL						

Greens in regulation

Front nine .... Back nine ....

Putting

First putts: short .... long .... holed ....

Second putts: short .... long .... holed ....

Bunkers

Fairway .... Greenside ....

Target reached .... Out in one shot ....

Penalties

Shots dropped: Hazards .... OoB ....

Up and downs

From rough .... From bunker .... From greenside ....

Best shot of the day

....

Most costly shot of the day

....

Positive points

....

What to avoid next time

....

Round 3

Course

Date   **Time**

Conditions

Tee/used competition

Hole	Par	Yards	Stroke index	Score	Drive	Putts
1						
2						
3						
4						
5						
6						
7						
8						
9						
10						
11						
12						
13						
14						
15						
16						
17						
18						
IN						
OUT						
TOTAL						

Greens in regulation

Front nine .... Back nine ....

Putting

First putts: short .... long .... holed.....................

Second putts: short .... long .... holed.....................

Bunkers

Fairway .... Greenside ....

Target reached .... Out in one shot..............................

Penalties

Shots dropped: Hazards .... OoB ....

Up and downs

From rough .... From bunker .... From greenside...............

Best shot of the day

....

Most costly shot of the day

....

Positive points

....

What to avoid next time

....

Round 4

Course

Date   **Time**

Conditions

Tee/used competition

Hole	Par	Yards	Stroke index	Score	Drive	Putts
1						
2						
3						
4						
5						
6						
7						
8						
9						
10						
11						
12						
13						
14						
15						
16						
17						
18						
IN						
OUT						
TOTAL						

Greens in regulation

Front nine .... Back nine ....

Putting

First putts: short .... long .... holed....................

Second putts: short .... long .... holed....................

Bunkers

Fairway .... Greenside ....

Target reached .... Out in one shot...............................

Penalties

Shots dropped: Hazards .... OoB....................................

Up and downs

From rough .... From bunker .... From greenside...............

Best shot of the day

....

Most costly shot of the day

....

Positive points

....

What to avoid next time

....

Round 5

Course

Date   **Time**

Conditions

Tee/used competition

Hole	Par	Yards	Stroke index	Score	Drive	Putts
1						
2						
3						
4						
5						
6						
7						
8						
9						
10						
11						
12						
13						
14						
15						
16						
17						
18						
IN						
OUT						
TOTAL						

Greens in regulation

Front nine .... Back nine ....

Putting

First putts: short .... long .... holed ....

Second putts: short .... long .... holed ....

Bunkers

Fairway .... Greenside ....

Target reached .... Out in one shot ....

Penalties

Shots dropped: Hazards .... OoB ....

Up and downs

From rough .... From bunker .... From greenside ....

Best shot of the day

....

Most costly shot of the day

....

Positive points

....

What to avoid next time

....

Round 6

Course

Date   Time

Conditions

Tee/used competition

Hole	Par	Yards	Stroke index	Score	Drive	Putts
1						
2						
3						
4						
5						
6						
7						
8						
9						
10						
11						
12						
13						
14						
15						
16						
17						
18						
IN						
OUT						
TOTAL						

Greens in regulation

Front nine.. Back nine...

Putting

First putts: short........................... long........................... holed.....................

Second putts: short..................... long......................... holed.....................

Bunkers

Fairway.. Greenside...

Target reached.................................... Out in one shot...............................

Penalties

Shots dropped: Hazards............................... OoB.....................................

Up and downs

From rough................ From bunker.................. From greenside...............

Best shot of the day

....

Most costly shot of the day

....

Positive points

....

What to avoid next time

....

Round 7

Course

Date	Time

Conditions

Tee/used competition

Hole	Par	Yards	Stroke index	Score	Drive	Putts
1						
2						
3						
4						
5						
6						
7						
8						
9						
10						
11						
12						
13						
14						
15						
16						
17						
18						
IN						
OUT						
TOTAL						

Greens in regulation

Front nine .... Back nine ....

Putting

First putts: short .... long .... holed ....

Second putts: short .... long .... holed ....

Bunkers

Fairway .... Greenside ....

Target reached .... Out in one shot ....

Penalties

Shots dropped: Hazards .... OoB ....

Up and downs

From rough .... From bunker .... From greenside ....

Best shot of the day

....

Most costly shot of the day

....

Positive points

....

What to avoid next time

....

Round 8

Course

Date   Time

Conditions

Tee/used competition

Hole	Par	Yards	Stroke index	Score	Drive	Putts
1						
2						
3						
4						
5						
6						
7						
8						
9						
10						
11						
12						
13						
14						
15						
16						
17						
18						
IN						
OUT						
TOTAL						

Greens in regulation

Front nine .... Back nine ....

Putting

First putts: short .... long .... holed.....................

Second putts: short .... long .... holed.....................

Bunkers

Fairway.. Greenside ....

Target reached .... Out in one shot................................

Penalties

Shots dropped: Hazards .... OoB.......................................

Up and downs

From rough .... From bunker .... From greenside...............

Best shot of the day

....

Most costly shot of the day

....

Positive points

....

What to avoid next time

....

Round 9

Course

Date   Time

Conditions

Tee/used competition

Hole	Par	Yards	Stroke index	Score	Drive	Putts
1						
2						
3						
4						
5						
6						
7						
8						
9						
10						
11						
12						
13						
14						
15						
16						
17						
18						
IN						
OUT						
TOTAL						

Greens in regulation

Front nine .... Back nine ....

Putting

First putts: short .... long .... holed ....

Second putts: short .... long .... holed ....

Bunkers

Fairway .... Greenside ....

Target reached .... Out in one shot ....

Penalties

Shots dropped: Hazards .... OoB ....

Up and downs

From rough .... From bunker .... From greenside ....

Best shot of the day

....

Most costly shot of the day

....

Positive points

....

What to avoid next time

....

Round 10

Course	
Date	Time
Conditions	
Tee/used competition	

Hole	Par	Yards	Stroke index	Score	Drive	Putts
1						
2						
3						
4						
5						
6						
7						
8						
9						
10						
11						
12						
13						
14						
15						
16						
17						
18						
IN						
OUT						
TOTAL						

Greens in regulation

Front nine .... Back nine ....

Putting

First putts: short .... long .... holed ....

Second putts: short .... long .... holed ....

Bunkers

Fairway .... Greenside ....

Target reached .... Out in one shot ....

Penalties

Shots dropped: Hazards .... OoB ....

Up and downs

From rough .... From bunker .... From greenside ....

Best shot of the day

....

Most costly shot of the day

....

Positive points

....

What to avoid next time

....

Analysis 1: rounds 1–10

ROUND	1	2	3	4	5	6	7	8	9	10
+/- net										
Total pars and better										
Total double bogeys or worse										
Shots lost to hazards and OoB										

ROUND	1	2	3	4	5	6	7	8	9	10
Fairways hit										
Greens in regulation										
Three putts or more										
Bunker shots successful										

Average net score over 10 rounds (+/-)	Best score	Worst score

My observations

Trends: Stableford analysis

ROUND	1	2	3	4	5	6	7	8	9	10
Hole										
1										
2										
3										
4										
5										
6										
7										
8										
9										
10										
11										
12										
13										
14										
15										
16										
17										
18										
Total points										

ROUND	1	2	3	4	5	6	7	8	9	10
Average score in first six holes										
Average score in second six holes										
Average score in third six holes										

Best run of net pars or better	Points between best and worst score

Round 11

Course

Date   Time

Conditions

Tee/used competition

Hole	Par	Yards	Stroke index	Score	Drive	Putts
1						
2						
3						
4						
5						
6						
7						
8						
9						
10						
11						
12						
13						
14						
15						
16						
17						
18						
IN						
OUT						
TOTAL						

Greens in regulation

Front nine .... Back nine ....

Putting

First putts: short .... long .... holed.....................

Second putts: short .... long .... holed.....................

Bunkers

Fairway .... Greenside ....

Target reached .... Out in one shot...............................

Penalties

Shots dropped: Hazards .... OoB.....................................

Up and downs

From rough .... From bunker .... From greenside...............

Best shot of the day

....

Most costly shot of the day

....

Positive points

....

What to avoid next time

....

Round 12

Course

Date   Time

Conditions

Tee/used competition

Hole	Par	Yards	Stroke index	Score	Drive	Putts
1						
2						
3						
4						
5						
6						
7						
8						
9						
10						
11						
12						
13						
14						
15						
16						
17						
18						
IN						
OUT						
TOTAL						

Greens in regulation

Front nine .... Back nine..

Putting

First putts: short .... long .... holed.....................

Second putts: short .... long .... holed.....................

Bunkers

Fairway... Greenside...

Target reached .... Out in one shot...............................

Penalties

Shots dropped: Hazards .... OoB.....................................

Up and downs

From rough .... From bunker .... From greenside...............

Best shot of the day

....

Most costly shot of the day

....

Positive points

....

What to avoid next time

....

Round 13

Course

Date   Time

Conditions

Tee/used competition

Hole	Par	Yards	Stroke index	Score	Drive	Putts
1						
2						
3						
4						
5						
6						
7						
8						
9						
10						
11						
12						
13						
14						
15						
16						
17						
18						
IN						
OUT						
TOTAL						

Greens in regulation

Front nine .... Back nine ....

Putting

First putts: short .... long .... holed.....................

Second putts: short .... long .... holed.....................

Bunkers

Fairway .... Greenside ....

Target reached .... Out in one shot..............................

Penalties

Shots dropped: Hazards .... OoB ....

Up and downs

From rough .... From bunker .... From greenside...............

Best shot of the day

....

Most costly shot of the day

....

Positive points

....

What to avoid next time

....

Round 14

Course

Date   Time

Conditions

Tee/used competition

Hole	Par	Yards	Stroke index	Score	Drive	Putts
1						
2						
3						
4						
5						
6						
7						
8						
9						
10						
11						
12						
13						
14						
15						
16						
17						
18						
IN						
OUT						
TOTAL						

Greens in regulation

Front nine.. Back nine..

Putting

First putts: short.......................... long......................... holed....................

Second putts: short.................... long......................... holed....................

Bunkers

Fairway.. Greenside.......................................

Target reached.................................... Out in one shot..............................

Penalties

Shots dropped: Hazards .... OoB....................................

Up and downs

From rough .... From bunker .... From greenside..............

Best shot of the day

....

Most costly shot of the day

....

Positive points

....

What to avoid next time

....

Round 15

Course

Date   Time

Conditions

Tee/used competition

Hole	Par	Yards	Stroke index	Score	Drive	Putts
1						
2						
3						
4						
5						
6						
7						
8						
9						
10						
11						
12						
13						
14						
15						
16						
17						
18						
IN						
OUT						
TOTAL						

Greens in regulation

Front nine .... Back nine ....

Putting

First putts: short .... long .... holed ....

Second putts: short .... long .... holed ....

Bunkers

Fairway .... Greenside ....

Target reached .... Out in one shot ....

Penalties

Shots dropped: Hazards .... OoB ....

Up and downs

From rough .... From bunker .... From greenside ....

Best shot of the day

....

Most costly shot of the day

....

Positive points

....

What to avoid next time

....

Round 16

Course

Date　　　　　　　　　　　**Time**

Conditions

Tee/used competition

Hole	Par	Yards	Stroke index	Score	Drive	Putts
1						
2						
3						
4						
5						
6						
7						
8						
9						
10						
11						
12						
13						
14						
15						
16						
17						
18						
IN						
OUT						
TOTAL						

Greens in regulation

Front nine .... Back nine..

Putting

First putts: short .... long .... holed....................

Second putts: short .... long .... holed....................

Bunkers

Fairway... Greenside.......................................

Target reached .... Out in one shot.............................

Penalties

Shots dropped: Hazards .... OoB....................................

Up and downs

From rough .... From bunker .... From greenside..............

Best shot of the day

....

Most costly shot of the day

....

Positive points

....

What to avoid next time

....

Round 17

Course	
Date	Time
Conditions	
Tee/used competition	

Hole	Par	Yards	Stroke index	Score	Drive	Putts
1						
2						
3						
4						
5						
6						
7						
8						
9						
10						
11						
12						
13						
14						
15						
16						
17						
18						
IN						
OUT						
TOTAL						

Greens in regulation

Front nine .... Back nine ....

Putting

First putts: short .... long .... holed.....................

Second putts: short .... long .... holed.....................

Bunkers

Fairway .... Greenside ....

Target reached .... Out in one shot ....

Penalties

Shots dropped: Hazards .... OoB ....

Up and downs

From rough .... From bunker .... From greenside ....

Best shot of the day

....

Most costly shot of the day

....

Positive points

....

What to avoid next time

....

Round 18

Course

Date   Time

Conditions

Tee/used competition

Hole	Par	Yards	Stroke index	Score	Drive	Putts
1						
2						
3						
4						
5						
6						
7						
8						
9						
10						
11						
12						
13						
14						
15						
16						
17						
18						
IN						
OUT						
TOTAL						

Greens in regulation

Front nine .... Back nine ....

Putting

First putts: short .... long .... holed.....................

Second putts: short .... long .... holed.....................

Bunkers

Fairway.. Greenside ....

Target reached .... Out in one shot...............................

Penalties

Shots dropped: Hazards .... OoB ....

Up and downs

From rough .... From bunker .... From greenside..............

Best shot of the day

....

Most costly shot of the day

....

Positive points

....

What to avoid next time

....

Round 19

Course

Date   **Time**

Conditions

Tee/used competition

Hole	Par	Yards	Stroke index	Score	Drive	Putts
1						
2						
3						
4						
5						
6						
7						
8						
9						
10						
11						
12						
13						
14						
15						
16						
17						
18						
IN						
OUT						
TOTAL						

Greens in regulation

Front nine .... Back nine ....

Putting

First putts: short .... long .... holed.....................

Second putts: short .... long .... holed.....................

Bunkers

Fairway.. Greenside ....

Target reached .... Out in one shot...............................

Penalties

Shots dropped: Hazards .... OoB....................................

Up and downs

From rough .... From bunker .... From greenside...............

Best shot of the day

....

Most costly shot of the day

....

Positive points

....

What to avoid next time

....

Round 20

Course

Date   Time

Conditions

Tee/used competition

Hole	Par	Yards	Stroke index	Score	Drive	Putts
1						
2						
3						
4						
5						
6						
7						
8						
9						
10						
11						
12						
13						
14						
15						
16						
17						
18						
IN						
OUT						
TOTAL						

Greens in regulation

Front nine .... Back nine ....

Putting

First putts: short .... long .... holed....................

Second putts: short .... long .... holed.....................

Bunkers

Fairway... Greenside ....

Target reached .... Out in one shot...............................

Penalties

Shots dropped: Hazards .... OoB....................................

Up and downs

From rough .... From bunker .... From greenside...............

Best shot of the day

....

Most costly shot of the day

....

Positive points

....

What to avoid next time

....

Analysis 2: rounds 11–20

ROUND	1	2	3	4	5	6	7	8	9	10
+/- net										
Total pars and better										
Total double bogeys or worse										
Shots lost to hazards and OoB										

ROUND	1	2	3	4	5	6	7	8	9	10
Fairways hit										
Greens in regulation										
Three putts or more										
Bunker shots successful										

Average net score over 10 rounds (+/-)	Best score	Worst score

My observations

Trends: Stableford analysis

ROUND	1	2	3	4	5	6	7	8	9	10
Hole										
1										
2										
3										
4										
5										
6										
7										
8										
9										
10										
11										
12										
13										
14										
15										
16										
17										
18										
Total points										

ROUND	1	2	3	4	5	6	7	8	9	10
Average score in first six holes										
Average score in second six holes										
Average score in third six holes										

Best run of net pars or better	Points between best and worst score

Round 21

Course

Date   Time

Conditions

Tee/used competition

Hole	Par	Yards	Stroke index	Score	Drive	Putts
1						
2						
3						
4						
5						
6						
7						
8						
9						
10						
11						
12						
13						
14						
15						
16						
17						
18						
IN						
OUT						
TOTAL						

Greens in regulation

Front nine .... Back nine ....

Putting

First putts: short .... long .... holed ....

Second putts: short .... long .... holed ....

Bunkers

Fairway .... Greenside ....

Target reached .... Out in one shot ....

Penalties

Shots dropped: Hazards .... OoB ....

Up and downs

From rough .... From bunker .... From greenside ....

Best shot of the day

....

Most costly shot of the day

....

Positive points

....

What to avoid next time

....

Round 22

Course

Date	Time

Conditions

Tee/used competition

Hole	Par	Yards	Stroke index	Score	Drive	Putts
1						
2						
3						
4						
5						
6						
7						
8						
9						
10						
11						
12						
13						
14						
15						
16						
17						
18						
IN						
OUT						
TOTAL						

Greens in regulation

Front nine .... Back nine ....

Putting

First putts: short .... long .... holed ....

Second putts: short .... long .... holed ....

Bunkers

Fairway .... Greenside ....

Target reached .... Out in one shot ....

Penalties

Shots dropped: Hazards .... OoB ....

Up and downs

From rough .... From bunker .... From greenside ....

Best shot of the day

....

Most costly shot of the day

....

Positive points

....

What to avoid next time

....

Round 23

Course

Date   **Time**

Conditions

Tee/used competition

Hole	Par	Yards	Stroke index	Score	Drive	Putts
1						
2						
3						
4						
5						
6						
7						
8						
9						
10						
11						
12						
13						
14						
15						
16						
17						
18						
IN						
OUT						
TOTAL						

Greens in regulation

Front nine .... Back nine ....

Putting

First putts: short .... long .... holed ....

Second putts: short .... long .... holed ....

Bunkers

Fairway .... Greenside ....

Target reached .... Out in one shot ....

Penalties

Shots dropped: Hazards .... OoB ....

Up and downs

From rough .... From bunker .... From greenside ....

Best shot of the day

....

Most costly shot of the day

....

Positive points

....

What to avoid next time

....

Round 24

Course

Date   **Time**

Conditions

Tee/used competition

Hole	Par	Yards	Stroke index	Score	Drive	Putts
1						
2						
3						
4						
5						
6						
7						
8						
9						
10						
11						
12						
13						
14						
15						
16						
17						
18						
IN						
OUT						
TOTAL						

Greens in regulation

Front nine .... Back nine ....

Putting

First putts: short .... long .... holed ....

Second putts: short .... long .... holed ....

Bunkers

Fairway .... Greenside ....

Target reached .... Out in one shot ....

Penalties

Shots dropped: Hazards .... OoB ....

Up and downs

From rough .... From bunker .... From greenside ....

Best shot of the day

....

Most costly shot of the day

....

Positive points

....

What to avoid next time

....

Round 25

Course

Date   **Time**

Conditions

Tee/used competition

Hole	Par	Yards	Stroke index	Score	Drive	Putts
1						
2						
3						
4						
5						
6						
7						
8						
9						
10						
11						
12						
13						
14						
15						
16						
17						
18						
IN						
OUT						
TOTAL						

Greens in regulation

Front nine .... Back nine ....

Putting

First putts: short .... long .... holed....................

Second putts: short .... long .... holed.....................

Bunkers

Fairway .... Greenside ....

Target reached .... Out in one shot.............................

Penalties

Shots dropped: Hazards .... OoB....................................

Up and downs

From rough .... From bunker .... From greenside...............

Best shot of the day

....

Most costly shot of the day

....

Positive points

....

What to avoid next time

....

Round 26

Course

Date   Time

Conditions

Tee/used competition

Hole	Par	Yards	Stroke index	Score	Drive	Putts
1						
2						
3						
4						
5						
6						
7						
8						
9						
10						
11						
12						
13						
14						
15						
16						
17						
18						
IN						
OUT						
TOTAL						

Greens in regulation

Front nine .... Back nine ....

Putting

First putts: short .... long .... holed ....

Second putts: short .... long .... holed ....

Bunkers

Fairway .... Greenside ....

Target reached .... Out in one shot ....

Penalties

Shots dropped: Hazards .... OoB ....

Up and downs

From rough .... From bunker .... From greenside ....

Best shot of the day

....

Most costly shot of the day

....

Positive points

....

What to avoid next time

....

Round 27

Course

Date   Time

Conditions

Tee/used competition

Hole	Par	Yards	Stroke index	Score	Drive	Putts
1						
2						
3						
4						
5						
6						
7						
8						
9						
10						
11						
12						
13						
14						
15						
16						
17						
18						
IN						
OUT						
TOTAL						

Greens in regulation

Front nine .... Back nine ....

Putting

First putts: short .... long .... holed ....

Second putts: short .... long .... holed ....

Bunkers

Fairway .... Greenside ....

Target reached .... Out in one shot ....

Penalties

Shots dropped: Hazards .... OoB ....

Up and downs

From rough .... From bunker .... From greenside ....

Best shot of the day

....

Most costly shot of the day

....

Positive points

....

What to avoid next time

....

Round 28

Course

Date   Time

Conditions

Tee/used competition

Hole	Par	Yards	Stroke index	Score	Drive	Putts
1						
2						
3						
4						
5						
6						
7						
8						
9						
10						
11						
12						
13						
14						
15						
16						
17						
18						
IN						
OUT						
TOTAL						

Greens in regulation

Front nine .... Back nine ....

Putting

First putts: short .... long .... holed.....................

Second putts: short .... long .... holed.....................

Bunkers

Fairway .... Greenside ....

Target reached .... Out in one shot...............................

Penalties

Shots dropped: Hazards .... OoB ....

Up and downs

From rough .... From bunker .... From greenside...............

Best shot of the day

....

Most costly shot of the day

....

Positive points

....

What to avoid next time

....

Round 29

Course

Date   **Time**

Conditions

Tee/used competition

Hole	Par	Yards	Stroke index	Score	Drive	Putts
1						
2						
3						
4						
5						
6						
7						
8						
9						
10						
11						
12						
13						
14						
15						
16						
17						
18						
IN						
OUT						
TOTAL						

Greens in regulation

Front nine .... Back nine.......................................

Putting

First putts: short .... long .... holed....................

Second putts: short .... long .... holed....................

Bunkers

Fairway... Greenside.......................................

Target reached .... Out in one shot.............................

Penalties

Shots dropped: Hazards .... OoB....................................

Up and downs

From rough .... From bunker .... From greenside...............

Best shot of the day

....

Most costly shot of the day

....

Positive points

....

What to avoid next time

....

Round 30

Course

Date				Time		

Conditions

Tee/used competition

Hole	Par	Yards	Stroke index	Score	Drive	Putts
1						
2						
3						
4						
5						
6						
7						
8						
9						
10						
11						
12						
13						
14						
15						
16						
17						
18						
IN						
OUT						
TOTAL						

Greens in regulation

Front nine .... Back nine ....

Putting

First putts: short .... long .... holed ....

Second putts: short .... long .... holed ....

Bunkers

Fairway .... Greenside ....

Target reached .... Out in one shot ....

Penalties

Shots dropped: Hazards .... OoB ....

Up and downs

From rough .... From bunker .... From greenside ....

Best shot of the day

....

Most costly shot of the day

....

Positive points

....

What to avoid next time

....

Analysis 3: rounds 21–30

ROUND	1	2	3	4	5	6	7	8	9	10
+/- net										
Total pars and better										
Total double bogeys or worse										
Shots lost to hazards and OoB										

ROUND	1	2	3	4	5	6	7	8	9	10
Fairways hit										
Greens in regulation										
Three putts or more										
Bunker shots successful										

Average net score over 10 rounds (+/-)	Best score	Worst score

My observations

Trends: Stableford analysis

ROUND	1	2	3	4	5	6	7	8	9	10
Hole										
1										
2										
3										
4										
5										
6										
7										
8										
9										
10										
11										
12										
13										
14										
15										
16										
17										
18										
Total points										

ROUND	1	2	3	4	5	6	7	8	9	10
Average score in first six holes										
Average score in second six holes										
Average score in third six holes										

Best run of net pars or better

Points between best and worst score

Round 31

Course

Date   **Time**

Conditions

Tee/used competition

Hole	Par	Yards	Stroke index	Score	Drive	Putts
1						
2						
3						
4						
5						
6						
7						
8						
9						
10						
11						
12						
13						
14						
15						
16						
17						
18						
IN						
OUT						
TOTAL						

Greens in regulation

Front nine .... Back nine ....

Putting

First putts: short .... long .... holed ....

Second putts: short .... long .... holed ....

Bunkers

Fairway .... Greenside ....

Target reached .... Out in one shot ....

Penalties

Shots dropped: Hazards .... OoB ....

Up and downs

From rough .... From bunker .... From greenside ....

Best shot of the day

....

Most costly shot of the day

....

Positive points

....

What to avoid next time

....

Round 32

Course

Date   **Time**

Conditions

Tee/used competition

Hole	Par	Yards	Stroke index	Score	Drive	Putts
1						
2						
3						
4						
5						
6						
7						
8						
9						
10						
11						
12						
13						
14						
15						
16						
17						
18						
IN						
OUT						
TOTAL						

Greens in regulation

Front nine .... Back nine ....

Putting

First putts: short .... long .... holed....................

Second putts: short .... long .... holed.....................

Bunkers

Fairway .... Greenside ....

Target reached .... Out in one shot..............................

Penalties

Shots dropped: Hazards .... OoB....................................

Up and downs

From rough .... From bunker .... From greenside...............

Best shot of the day

....

Most costly shot of the day

....

Positive points

....

What to avoid next time

....

Round 33

Course

Date   Time

Conditions

Tee/used competition

Hole	Par	Yards	Stroke index	Score	Drive	Putts
1						
2						
3						
4						
5						
6						
7						
8						
9						
10						
11						
12						
13						
14						
15						
16						
17						
18						
IN						
OUT						
TOTAL						

Greens in regulation

Front nine.. Back nine...

Putting

First putts: short.......................... long .... holed...................

Second putts: short .... long .... holed....................

Bunkers

Fairway.. Greenside...

Target reached .... Out in one shot...............................

Penalties

Shots dropped: Hazards .... OoB...

Up and downs

From rough .... From bunker .... From greenside...............

Best shot of the day

....

Most costly shot of the day

....

Positive points

....

What to avoid next time

....

Round 34

Course

Date   Time

Conditions

Tee/used competition

Hole	Par	Yards	Stroke index	Score	Drive	Putts
1						
2						
3						
4						
5						
6						
7						
8						
9						
10						
11						
12						
13						
14						
15						
16						
17						
18						
IN						
OUT						
TOTAL						

Greens in regulation

Front nine .... Back nine ....

Putting

First putts: short .... long .... holed...................

Second putts: short .... long .... holed.....................

Bunkers

Fairway .... Greenside ....

Target reached .... Out in one shot...............................

Penalties

Shots dropped: Hazards .... OoB...

Up and downs

From rough .... From bunker .... From greenside...............

Best shot of the day

....

Most costly shot of the day

....

Positive points

....

What to avoid next time

....

Round 35

Course	
Date	Time
Conditions	
Tee/used competition	

Hole	Par	Yards	Stroke index	Score	Drive	Putts
1						
2						
3						
4						
5						
6						
7						
8						
9						
10						
11						
12						
13						
14						
15						
16						
17						
18						
IN						
OUT						
TOTAL						

Greens in regulation

Front nine .... Back nine ....

Putting

First putts: short .... long .... holed.....................

Second putts: short .... long .... holed.....................

Bunkers

Fairway.. Greenside ....

Target reached .... Out in one shot...............................

Penalties

Shots dropped: Hazards .... OoB.....................................

Up and downs

From rough .... From bunker .... From greenside...............

Best shot of the day

....

Most costly shot of the day

....

Positive points

....

What to avoid next time

....

Round 36

Course

Date   Time

Conditions

Tee/used competition

Hole	Par	Yards	Stroke index	Score	Drive	Putts
1						
2						
3						
4						
5						
6						
7						
8						
9						
10						
11						
12						
13						
14						
15						
16						
17						
18						
IN						
OUT						
TOTAL						

Greens in regulation

Front nine .... Back nine ....

Putting

First putts: short .... long .... holed ....

Second putts: short .... long .... holed ....

Bunkers

Fairway .... Greenside ....

Target reached .... Out in one shot ....

Penalties

Shots dropped: Hazards .... OoB ....

Up and downs

From rough .... From bunker .... From greenside ....

Best shot of the day

....

Most costly shot of the day

....

Positive points

....

What to avoid next time

....

Round 37

Course
Date   Time
Conditions
Tee/used competition

Hole	Par	Yards	Stroke index	Score	Drive	Putts
1						
2						
3						
4						
5						
6						
7						
8						
9						
10						
11						
12						
13						
14						
15						
16						
17						
18						
IN						
OUT						
TOTAL						

Greens in regulation

Front nine .... Back nine ....

Putting

First putts: short .... long .... holed.....................

Second putts: short .... long .... holed.....................

Bunkers

Fairway.. Greenside...

Target reached .... Out in one shot..............................

Penalties

Shots dropped: Hazards .... OoB......................................

Up and downs

From rough .... From bunker .... From greenside..............

Best shot of the day

....

Most costly shot of the day

....

Positive points

....

What to avoid next time

....

Round 38

Course

Date   Time

Conditions

Tee/used competition

Hole	Par	Yards	Stroke index	Score	Drive	Putts
1						
2						
3						
4						
5						
6						
7						
8						
9						
10						
11						
12						
13						
14						
15						
16						
17						
18						
IN						
OUT						
TOTAL						

Greens in regulation

Front nine .... Back nine ....

Putting

First putts: short .... long .... holed ....

Second putts: short .... long .... holed ....

Bunkers

Fairway .... Greenside ....

Target reached .... Out in one shot ....

Penalties

Shots dropped: Hazards .... OoB ....

Up and downs

From rough .... From bunker .... From greenside ....

Best shot of the day

....

Most costly shot of the day

....

Positive points

....

What to avoid next time

....

Round 39

Course

Date   Time

Conditions

Tee/used competition

Hole	Par	Yards	Stroke index	Score	Drive	Putts
1						
2						
3						
4						
5						
6						
7						
8						
9						
10						
11						
12						
13						
14						
15						
16						
17						
18						
IN						
OUT						
TOTAL						

Greens in regulation

Front nine .... Back nine ....

Putting

First putts: short .... long .... holed.....................

Second putts: short .... long .... holed.....................

Bunkers

Fairway .... Greenside ....

Target reached .... Out in one shot ....

Penalties

Shots dropped: Hazards .... OoB ....

Up and downs

From rough .... From bunker .... From greenside...............

Best shot of the day

....

Most costly shot of the day

....

Positive points

....

What to avoid next time

....

Round 40

Course

Date   **Time**

Conditions

Tee/used competition

Hole	Par	Yards	Stroke index	Score	Drive	Putts
1						
2						
3						
4						
5						
6						
7						
8						
9						
10						
11						
12						
13						
14						
15						
16						
17						
18						
IN						
OUT						
TOTAL						

Greens in regulation

Front nine .... Back nine ....

Putting

First putts: short .... long .... holed....................

Second putts: short .... long .... holed....................

Bunkers

Fairway... Greenside ....

Target reached .... Out in one shot..............................

Penalties

Shots dropped: Hazards .... OoB....................................

Up and downs

From rough .... From bunker .... From greenside...............

Best shot of the day

....

Most costly shot of the day

....

Positive points

....

What to avoid next time

....

Analysis 4: rounds 31–40

ROUND	1	2	3	4	5	6	7	8	9	10
+/- net										
Total pars and better										
Total double bogeys or worse										
Shots lost to hazards and OoB										

ROUND	1	2	3	4	5	6	7	8	9	10
Fairways hit										
Greens in regulation										
Three putts or more										
Bunker shots successful										

Average net score over 10 rounds (+/-)	Best score	Worst score

My observations

Trends: Stableford analysis

ROUND	1	2	3	4	5	6	7	8	9	10
Hole										
1										
2										
3										
4										
5										
6										
7										
8										
9										
10										
11										
12										
13										
14										
15										
16										
17										
18										
Total points										

ROUND	1	2	3	4	5	6	7	8	9	10
Average score in first six holes										
Average score in second six holes										
Average score in third six holes										

Best run of net pars or better	Points between best and worst score

Round 41

Course

Date   Time

Conditions

Tee/used competition

Hole	Par	Yards	Stroke index	Score	Drive	Putts
1						
2						
3						
4						
5						
6						
7						
8						
9						
10						
11						
12						
13						
14						
15						
16						
17						
18						
IN						
OUT						
TOTAL						

Greens in regulation

Front nine .... Back nine...

Putting

First putts: short............................ long .... holed....................

Second putts: short .... long .... holed....................

Bunkers

Fairway.. Greenside ....

Target reached .... Out in one shot...............................

Penalties

Shots dropped: Hazards .... OoB.....................................

Up and downs

From rough .... From bunker .... From greenside...............

Best shot of the day

....

Most costly shot of the day

....

Positive points

....

What to avoid next time

....

Round 42

Course

Date   Time

Conditions

Tee/used competition

Hole	Par	Yards	Stroke index	Score	Drive	Putts
1						
2						
3						
4						
5						
6						
7						
8						
9						
10						
11						
12						
13						
14						
15						
16						
17						
18						
IN						
OUT						
TOTAL						

Greens in regulation

Front nine .... Back nine ....

Putting

First putts: short .... long .... holed....................

Second putts: short .... long .... holed....................

Bunkers

Fairway.. Greenside ....

Target reached .... Out in one shot..............................

Penalties

Shots dropped: Hazards .... OoB....................................

Up and downs

From rough .... From bunker .... From greenside...............

Best shot of the day

....

Most costly shot of the day

....

Positive points

....

What to avoid next time

....

Round 43

Course

Date   Time

Conditions

Tee/used competition

Hole	Par	Yards	Stroke index	Score	Drive	Putts
1						
2						
3						
4						
5						
6						
7						
8						
9						
10						
11						
12						
13						
14						
15						
16						
17						
18						
IN						
OUT						
TOTAL						

Greens in regulation

Front nine .... Back nine ....

Putting

First putts: short .... long .... holed.....................

Second putts: short .... long .... holed.....................

Bunkers

Fairway .... Greenside ....

Target reached .... Out in one shot...............................

Penalties

Shots dropped: Hazards .... OoB....................................

Up and downs

From rough .... From bunker .... From greenside...............

Best shot of the day

....

Most costly shot of the day

....

Positive points

....

What to avoid next time

....

Round 44

Course

Date   Time

Conditions

Tee/used competition

Hole	Par	Yards	Stroke index	Score	Drive	Putts
1						
2						
3						
4						
5						
6						
7						
8						
9						
10						
11						
12						
13						
14						
15						
16						
17						
18						
IN						
OUT						
TOTAL						

Greens in regulation

Front nine .... Back nine ....

Putting

First putts: short .... long .... holed.....................

Second putts: short .... long .... holed.....................

Bunkers

Fairway.. Greenside ....

Target reached .... Out in one shot...............................

Penalties

Shots dropped: Hazards .... OoB.......................................

Up and downs

From rough .... From bunker .... From greenside...............

Best shot of the day

....

Most costly shot of the day

....

Positive points

....

What to avoid next time

....

Round 45

Course

Date   Time

Conditions

Tee/used competition

Hole	Par	Yards	Stroke index	Score	Drive	Putts
1						
2						
3						
4						
5						
6						
7						
8						
9						
10						
11						
12						
13						
14						
15						
16						
17						
18						
IN						
OUT						
TOTAL						

Greens in regulation

Front nine .... Back nine ....

Putting

First putts: short .... long .... holed ....

Second putts: short .... long .... holed ....

Bunkers

Fairway .... Greenside ....

Target reached .... Out in one shot ....

Penalties

Shots dropped: Hazards .... OoB ....

Up and downs

From rough .... From bunker .... From greenside ....

Best shot of the day

....

Most costly shot of the day

....

Positive points

....

What to avoid next time

....

Round 46

Course

Date   Time

Conditions

Tee/used competition

Hole	Par	Yards	Stroke index	Score	Drive	Putts
1						
2						
3						
4						
5						
6						
7						
8						
9						
10						
11						
12						
13						
14						
15						
16						
17						
18						
IN						
OUT						
TOTAL						

Greens in regulation

Front nine .... Back nine...

Putting

First putts: short .... long .... holed.....................

Second putts: short .... long .... holed.....................

Bunkers

Fairway... Greenside ....

Target reached .... Out in one shot...............................

Penalties

Shots dropped: Hazards .... OoB.....................................

Up and downs

From rough .... From bunker .... From greenside...............

Best shot of the day

....

Most costly shot of the day

....

Positive points

....

What to avoid next time

....

Round 47

Course

Date   Time

Conditions

Tee/used competition

Hole	Par	Yards	Stroke index	Score	Drive	Putts
1						
2						
3						
4						
5						
6						
7						
8						
9						
10						
11						
12						
13						
14						
15						
16						
17						
18						
IN						
OUT						
TOTAL						

Greens in regulation

Front nine .... Back nine ....

Putting

First putts: short .... long .... holed ....

Second putts: short .... long .... holed ....

Bunkers

Fairway .... Greenside ....

Target reached .... Out in one shot ....

Penalties

Shots dropped: Hazards .... OoB ....

Up and downs

From rough .... From bunker .... From greenside ....

Best shot of the day

....

Most costly shot of the day

....

Positive points

....

What to avoid next time

....

Round 48

Course

Date   Time

Conditions

Tee/used competition

Hole	Par	Yards	Stroke index	Score	Drive	Putts
1						
2						
3						
4						
5						
6						
7						
8						
9						
10						
11						
12						
13						
14						
15						
16						
17						
18						
IN						
OUT						
TOTAL						

Greens in regulation

Front nine .... Back nine ....

Putting

First putts: short .... long .... holed....................

Second putts: short .... long .... holed.....................

Bunkers

Fairway.. Greenside ....

Target reached .... Out in one shot...............................

Penalties

Shots dropped: Hazards .... OoB ....

Up and downs

From rough .... From bunker .... From greenside..............

Best shot of the day

....

Most costly shot of the day

....

Positive points

....

What to avoid next time

....

Round 49

Course

Date   Time

Conditions

Tee/used competition

Hole	Par	Yards	Stroke index	Score	Drive	Putts
1						
2						
3						
4						
5						
6						
7						
8						
9						
10						
11						
12						
13						
14						
15						
16						
17						
18						
IN						
OUT						
TOTAL						

Greens in regulation

Front nine .... Back nine ....

Putting

First putts: short .... long .... holed.....................

Second putts: short .... long .... holed.....................

Bunkers

Fairway... Greenside ....

Target reached .... Out in one shot................................

Penalties

Shots dropped: Hazards .... OoB ....

Up and downs

From rough .... From bunker .... From greenside...............

Best shot of the day

....

Most costly shot of the day

....

Positive points

....

What to avoid next time

....

Round 50

Course	
Date	Time
Conditions	
Tee/used competition	

Hole	Par	Yards	Stroke index	Score	Drive	Putts
1						
2						
3						
4						
5						
6						
7						
8						
9						
10						
11						
12						
13						
14						
15						
16						
17						
18						
IN						
OUT						
TOTAL						

Greens in regulation

Front nine .... Back nine ....

Putting

First putts: short .... long .... holed ....

Second putts: short .... long .... holed ....

Bunkers

Fairway .... Greenside ....

Target reached .... Out in one shot ....

Penalties

Shots dropped: Hazards .... OoB ....

Up and downs

From rough .... From bunker .... From greenside ....

Best shot of the day

....

Most costly shot of the day

....

Positive points

....

What to avoid next time

....

Analysis 5: rounds 41–50

ROUND	1	2	3	4	5	6	7	8	9	10
+/- net										
Total pars and better										
Total double bogeys or worse										
Shots lost to hazards and OoB										

ROUND	1	2	3	4	5	6	7	8	9	10
Fairways hit										
Greens in regulation										
Three putts or more										
Bunker shots successful										

Average net score over 10 rounds (+/-)

Best score

Worst score

My observations

Trends: Stableford analysis

ROUND	1	2	3	4	5	6	7	8	9	10
Hole										
1										
2										
3										
4										
5										
6										
7										
8										
9										
10										
11										
12										
13										
14										
15										
16										
17										
18										
Total points										

ROUND	1	2	3	4	5	6	7	8	9	10
Average score in first six holes										
Average score in second six holes										
Average score in third six holes										

Best run of net pars or better

Points between best and worst score

Fault fixer:
Improve your game

Driving distance Checking the width of your stance

Having the correct width of stance in the golf swing is vital when producing power. If you are too wide, your leg movement will be restricted and you won't be able to transfer your weight correctly. If the stance is too narrow, you will have a tendency to lose balance once the weight has been transferred. A good basic guide is to have your feet shoulder-width apart for a medium iron. Widen the stance slightly for longer clubs and narrow it slightly for shorter clubs. Width of stance is a different issue from width of backswing (see

Wide stance

The width issue applies to all clubs and all shots. This stance is too wide for the 6 iron used. The combination of wide stance and mid-iron will mean that, in order to have the hands correctly positioned, the ball will have to be placed too far from the body.

Narrow stance

The stance above is too narrow for the shot. With this stance and this club (6 iron), the stance will be too upright and a full swing will result in instability. You would have your feet this close together only for short shots around the green.

pages 134–135). Stance width, distance from the ball, and ball alignment will all change depending upon the club being used. As the club length lessens, from driver to wedge, the ball moves closer to the centre of the stance and the stance width decreases.

PRO TIP You may tend to swing harder with the longer clubs, so allow yourself a little extra width in the stance for improved balance.

REMEMBER

The loft of your driver may also make a difference to distance. They tend to vary from about 7–12 degrees. The general rule is that higher handicap players benefit more from greater loft. Try out the options on the practice ground.

Ideal stance
It is balance, facilitating a smooth swing, that helps create distance. A 6 iron, as seen above, should be played from slightly forward of centre. The ideal model for a 9 iron is to have the ball mid-stance and the feet approximately shoulder-width apart.

PRO TIP When you're on the course you tend to lose focus on the basics – worrying instead about your score or your opponent. A quick check of your stance may be rewarded with greater weight transference.

Driving distance Increasing your clubhead speed

Length and control

Clubhead speed is essentially what makes the ball travel further. The faster the club is travelling when it strikes the ball, the faster the ball will come off the face. The impact makes the ball stay in the air longer and, while the ball is in the air, it is going forwards. The problem with hitting the ball harder is the potential loss of control. The upside of being a shorter hitter is that, on average, you will hit it straighter than the person who gives 100 per cent every shot.

Luke Donald of England talks with his brother and caddie Christian during the final round of the Masters at Augusta. Top players have great control over their game and, as such, have more decisions to make than high-handicappers. Their "comfort zone" is very wide.

Finding the balance

The answer is that you need to find a balance, a point where you are generating enough clubhead speed to be able to get round a golf course, but also with enough accuracy not to lose shot after shot, or worse, ball after ball!

The key is to find your point of balance off the course, on the practice range. Only you will know where your comfort zone is – where you can hit the ball hard but with relative accuracy. Once you've found what suits you, you might be able to slowly increase your speed.

Clubhead speed

The only way of truly analysing clubhead speed is by using one of the many new computer systems that simulate actual play. Sophisticated systems can be very useful in helping you understand not only when you are accelerating, but also the shape and distance of your shot.

Swing analysis

You can use modern technology, such as a digital video camera or even a camera phone, to check your swing. Often the main difference between tour players and decent amateurs is the swing speed in the last few moments; pros release the wrists, bringing the club through very briskly.

PRO TIP Golf is about confidence. Your comfort zone should be where you can be confident of hitting the target most of the time. Don't push it too hard, too quickly.

Driving distance Adjusting the width of your backswing

Creating room

Width in the backswing is a big factor when creating extra power in the golf swing. Without width it becomes extremely difficult to drive into the ball using the whole of the body. There is simply not enough room to take the club back and bring it through.

Body movement

A swing that lacks width tends to restrict body movement. You have to use too much hand and arm action to try to speed up the club, resulting in loss of control and usually a strike with less power rather than more. Maintaining width through the downswing will

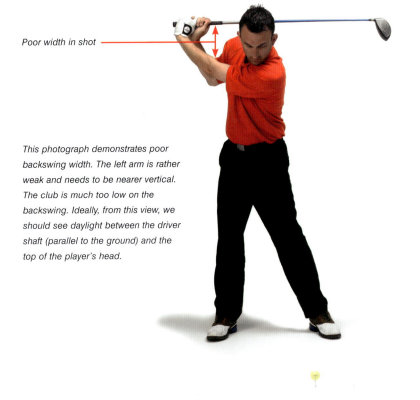

Poor width in shot

This photograph demonstrates poor backswing width. The left arm is rather weak and needs to be nearer vertical. The club is much too low on the backswing. Ideally, from this view, we should see daylight between the driver shaft (parallel to the ground) and the top of the player's head.

REMEMBER

For more confidence on the tee with your driver you need to feel comfortable with the ball/tee height. As a basic rule, tee the ball up so the middle of the clubhead is above the centre of the ball.

give you much more room through impact, thus allowing more of an attack with the body.

A wide position at the top of the back swing is the distance between the shaft and the player. This is crucial. The bigger this gap, the wider the swing arc.

PRO TIP When at the top of the backswing, stop and then try to push your hands towards the sky while maintaining posture, but don't straighten your back. This will create tightness in the backswing, and maintain width.

Good width in shot

David Toms hits his tee shot on the 12th hole during the final round of the Ford Championship at Doral, Florida. His left arm is thrown high providing plenty of width in his shot.

Wrong shape of tee shot
Weight transference, grip, and hand action

If you're not getting the shape you want from your tee shot, you need to think back to basics. The grip and hand action may be relatively easy to put right – but refining your weight transference may be the real key to improvement.

> **PRO TIP** The body should feel coiled on the backswing.

Check your grip

When you look down at your *grip*, check that:

- The two Vs created by the forefinger and thumb are pointing towards an area between your chin and right shoulder;
- The palms of the hands are facing each other.

At address the player should feel equal weight distribution between both feet, but have the weight slightly towards their toes (about 60%).

Once the back swing starts the player should start to feel the weight shifting 80% to the right foot and 20% towards the left toes.

Then when the shoulders start to rotate more, this will put the weight on the right heel (50%) and left toe (50%).

Check your hand action

With your *hand action*, as you go through your practice swings:

- during the take-away, if you stop the club when it is parallel to the ground you should see the toe of the club pointing upwards towards the sky;
- at the top of your backswing you should have created a 90° angle between the shaft and left arm.

Check your weight transference

Weight transference also plays a huge part in being able to control the clubface because the body needs to rotate as well as the hands through impact to ensure the clubface hits the ball squarely. The backswing needs to feel left-side dominant. The left shoulder turns and the left arm is drawn across the chest as it lifts. The left hand (for right-handers, of course) needs to feel in control.

The weight balance will remain constant as the player continues the backswing.

At the top of the swing, check that you are still keeping head still and eyes on the back of the ball. The maximum weight will be on the right foot, the left remaining grounded.

Fairways missed left Is your body in alignment?

When a ball veers off target you have to take into account how it got there. The main questions are:

- Where did the ball start?
- Where did the ball finish?

The first thing to check is your alignment. The feet, knees, hips, and shoulders must all be parallel to the ball-to-target line. If they are not, then this can seriously affect the swing plane.

Planes of alignment

It is a simple concept but one that is worth checking and checking again. The arrows show both the direction and the "plane" of the parts of the body. Not only is everything pointing the same way, but the hips, shoulders, and knees are all parallel.

The error here is clear to spot and rather overstated – but players do misalign to this degree, especially when lacking concentration. See also pages 166–167.

Placing a club on the ground in front of the feet, and then placing a club along the knees, hips, and shoulders, will give the player an indication of where they actually are aiming. This applies to hitting the ball both left and right of the fairway (see pages 140–149 and the alignment masterclass on pages 166–167).

REMEMBER

Alignment is key and twisting out of alignment can cause problems. However, remember that for short pitch shots, where you have the ball back in your stance, you may need to turn your feet to the left. As the diagram shows, you need to turn the back foot, too.

This is a very simple technique to help alignment. Place the club pointing directly parallel to the target and set your feet along the shaft. Check that your clubface is pointing at your target. You can use this procedure on the course, but you must pick up the club before the shot. If you leave the club, or any object, on the ground to help you align you will be breaking the rules.

PRO TIP Top players will choose their club, make their practice swings, and then, as the last routine before they play the shot, check their alignment.

Fairways missed left Ensuring your swing plane is correct

"Out-to-in" swing

This is a very simple diagram to demonstrate an important point. This "out-to-in" swing path will send the ball off towards the left. It may stay in that direction or, if the clubface is open at impact, the ball may eventually effect a slice/fade and end up right of the fairway. A closed clubface at this point will send the ball further left. Whatever the result, the out-to-in pattern will mean loss of control and distance.

The swing plane, the movement of the club from take-away through to finish, will determine where the ball starts. A swing that has a club shaft pointing left of the target at the top of the backswing will create an out-to-in swing path and cause the ball to start left of the target.

The correct position at the top of the backswing would show the shaft on exactly the same plane as your feet, knees, hips, and shoulders at address.

REMEMBER There are numerous ways of hitting the ball left.

The draw
A slightly closed clubface. A popular shape of shot if aimed right at the tee.

The pull hook
The ball starts left from an out-to-in swing with the added problem of a closed clubface.

The hook
The ball starts right from an in-to-out swing with a closed clubface, hit too far back in the stance.

The pull
A shot hit straight out to the left with a square face, perhaps hit too late in the swing path.

*David Toms, demonstrating
perfect swing shape, poise,
and focus, hits a shot
during an official practice
day for the 2006 Ryder Cup
at The K Club in Ireland.*

PRO TIP Using either a video camera or a friend, stop at the top of your backswing and ensure the shaft is pointing in the correct direction. Only you have control over the club.

Fairways missed left
Where's your clubface at the point of impact?

If the ball starts out towards the target, but then turns left, this is a different matter from just poor alignment or swing plane. This problem almost certainly lies in the clubface position, not the swing.

Clubface control

The clubface is controlled only by your hands, so to make the ball spin left the clubface must be "closed" at impact.

There are two common reasons for the problem:

- The grip is too strong initially. This means the two V-shapes you have created between both thumbs and forefingers are too much to the right of your chin.
- At some point during the swing the hands are closing the club; this can be done at various points during the swing. During the *backswing*, if the hands do not rotate enough, this will cause a closed position. Or, *on the downswing*, if the wrist is un-cocked too soon this will also cause the club to close.

Hitting left

Both of the faults shown on the left and right (strong grip and closing face) result in right-to-left spin being imparted on the ball and causing it to finish left of target. Another common result of a closed clubface is an early hit of the ball.

Strong grip

The strong grip shown here will mean the take-back and eventual shot will be closed or hooded which will result in a draw and lower flight. You have to be careful when watching professionals as they may intentionally create a strong grip to induce a draw or hook on the ball.

REMEMBER The club/ball interface is clearly the most important aspect of a shot. If this is right the ball will go straight. Try hard to visualize that perfectly aligned strike of club and ball. Aiming to send your ball over interim targets (say a hump or mark on the fairway) on the way to the eventual target can help your focus and direction.

PRO TIP When trying to isolate a fault, remember that *swing* determines the initial direction of the ball and *spin* determines the flight of the ball once it's in the air.

Closing face

Here the club has closed during the take-away and, unless the player takes remedial action, the club will hit the ball at an angle and hook it to the left.

Fairways missed right Lining up for the target

Alignment and the target

Setting your body in alignment to the target, of course, relates to both hitting left and right (see also pages 138–139). Being in alignment, however, is only half the problem. You may have everything pointing in the same direction, but is it the *right* direction? You may feel that you've just hit the ball perfectly but it goes wide of the target. The problem is probably your lining-up.

This is clearly a simple fault to correct, but it is one that may pay big rewards. You will have learned this when you had your first lessons – but do take time to check that the imaginary line drawn across your toes is actually parallel to the target.

PRO TIP Double and triple check body alignment, and then analyse your shot. It will become easier to realize whether it's an alignment, swing-related, or grip problem.

The set-up here is likely to generate left-to-right spin and a shot that misses the target to the right. The lines shown on the photograph need to be parallel.

Check your target

The other key point to remember, well worth mentioning here, is that the flag is rarely the target. As you line up for the shot, think about:

- avoiding hazards – going over or round them;
- gauging the amount of ball movement after landing – roll or backspin;
- the shape of the fairway or green – will the ball veer off?

Tiger Woods hits a shot from the fairway as his coach Hank Haney looks on during a practice round for the US Open Championship at Winged Foot. Having a friend or coach look at your set-up during practice can be invaluable. Set-up errors cost a lot of shots, but are very easy to rectify.

Fairways missed right Are you swinging "in-to-out"?

Just as with missing fairways on the left (see pages 140–141), it is possible that your swing plane is letting you down when you hit to the right. In this case you may be swinging in-to-out (an out-to-in plane means that you are likely to miss the fairway to the left).

Clubface or swing?

Once again, this can be either a clubface or a swing problem. The main position to check during the swing is at the point just before impact at waist height, if the club shaft is pointing right of target then this is proof of an in-to-out path.

This position will always start the ball to the right, however, even if the club shaft at this position is on line or even left of target, the ball can still finish right of target if the clubface is open enough to create side spin. Sometimes very simple remedies can be the solution, for example a player may be swinging the club very well, missing his/her target right every time, and may just have the clubface too open at address.

The body working as one

During the swing it is important to feel like the upper body (shoulders and arms) and lower body (legs and hips) work together. A common fault that causes shots to be lost to the right is where a player starts to drive with the legs and hips too soon, almost leaving the club behind and consequently not leaving the player with enough time or space to return the clubface squarely to the ball.

REMEMBER There are a number of names given to hitting the ball right.

The fade
The ball starts straight and falls away slightly to the right due to an open clubface.

The push fade
Produced by an in-to-out swing path with an open clubface pushing it further.

The slice
An out-to-in swing starts left, but the ball has been cut across as the face is open in relation to the swing.

The push
An in-to-out swing with a square face sends the ball straight but right.

PRO TIP Having either a mirror or a video camera is an excellent way of checking your swing plane alone.

It is quite useful, and advisable, to look back at your take-away during a practice swing. This not only checks your swing path, but reminds you of the line you want. Here, the player is ensuring that the face is neither too open or closed and that the swing plane is correct.

"In-to-out" swing

This simple diagram demonstrates the line taken in an in-to-out swing. This can result in fairways being missed both right and left depending upon the clubface at impact. The main problem with in-to-out or out-to-in paths is that players notice the effect and then introduce more swing errors in an attempt to compensate. Ask somebody to check your swing path (see page 145).

Fairways missed right
Weak grip or bad wrist angle

If your grip is weak rather than strong, there is a big danger of your missing the fairway to the right (see also pages 144–145). In a weak grip, the Vs between thumbs and forefinger will be pointing too far to the left of the chin. Check this out first.

Alternatively, if the ball is still going right, check the angle of the left wrist when bringing the club down into impact. If the cocking of your wrist has been held too long, this will result in an open clubface left-to-right spin.

Another common problem could be too much rotation in the wrist action during take-away. This will give you a very open clubface during the backswing and, once the club is very open, it becomes difficult to ever get it back square.

REMEMBER

The grip shown here is the **Vardon grip**, named after the American golfer Harry Vardon. It is characterized by the right hand little finger interlocking with the left hand index finger. The **Baseball grip** is where the hands are close together but not interlinking.

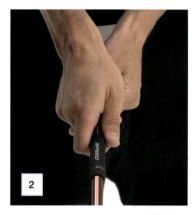

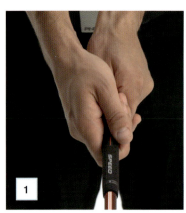

Neutral (1), weak (2), and strong (3) grips. The neutral grip is ideal for most shots although weak and strong grips can be deliberately chosen to effect fade (weak) and draw (strong) shots.

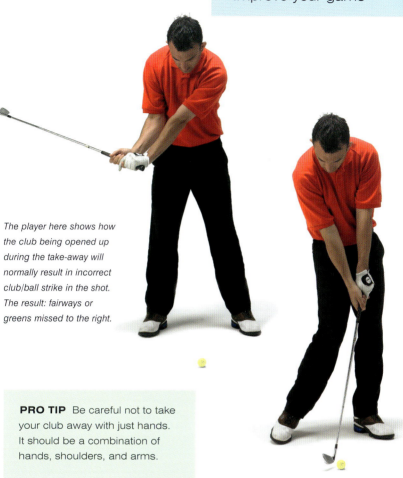

*The player here shows how
the club being opened up
during the take-away will
normally result in incorrect
club/ball strike in the shot.
The result: fairways or
greens missed to the right.*

PRO TIP Be careful not to take
your club away with just hands.
It should be a combination of
hands, shoulders, and arms.

Shanks

An open club at impact will impart
left to right spin and, if excessive,
may even bring on the dreaded
"shank" – a very angled shot out
to the right.

Par three greens
Choosing the right club

Obviously you are not expected to hit every par 3 green, every time, but you do have less excuse for missing because:

- the tee area is flat – a shot becomes more difficult when the ball is either above or below a player's feet;
- you have the exact yardage to the green centre – judgment isn't required as the distance is already shown on the card;
- the lie of the ball will be perfect (on a tee peg) – the more difficult the lie, the harder to control the strike and spin.

Club selection

The main reason for missing a par 3 green is that you have trouble with club selection. To ensure good club selection you need to "know your distances". For example, if you hit a 7 iron perfectly it might go 150 yards or, if you hit it poorly, it might go 130 yards. What do you base your selection on? The answer is the average, so you can expect your 7 iron to travel approximately 140 yards.

To be more accurate, go to the practice ground and hit balls with a certain club, then measure the average distance. You will soon work out how far, typically, you hit each club. Over a period of time you should do this with every club in your bag. When you're on the course, all you need is the yardage; the club selection is almost automatic.

Assess the trouble

You also need to assess the hole. If, for example, all the trouble is at the front it may be a wiser choice to hit a club that, even if you strike poorly, will clear the trouble. Check out all the trouble – and how far away it is. It's better to be just

over the green and above ground than just short but in a ditch. And vice versa, if there is danger at the back of the green choose a club that *can't* get there.

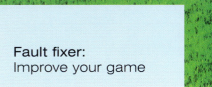

Fault fixer:
Improve your game

This page allows a chance to look again at the par 3, 17th hole at Sawgrass in Ponte Vedra Beach, Florida, in use for the Players' Championship. Good club selection – and confidence in the shot – are vital here. Amateur players may also need a good supply of balls.

PRO TIP When on a par 3 tee, don't just look at the yardage – see where the trouble is, and choose a club to stay away from the trouble. You can't really afford extra dropped shots on any hole, especially not on a par 3.

Par three greens
The angle of attack

Many golfers play the ball from close to the centre of the teeing area on every hole. This is not necessarily a good idea. Especially on par threes you should think about the angle of attack. By teeing up on the right hand side of the tee box you are hitting *away* from the right side of the hole and green. If the trouble is located right of the green then this would be a sensible option.

Also, for example, if the flag is located on the left side of the green then by teeing up on the right side this will open the flag up to being attacked. This will be

Deciding the angle of attack at a par three hole is the result of a number of decisions.

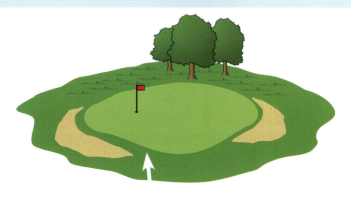

Does the green slope – back-to-front, side-to-side?

Is the green holding or will the ball bounce off?

Is this a matchplay shot? Has your opponent played yet?

How crucial is a par? Will your card be OK with a bogey?

How good a bunker player are you? Can you afford to be in the bunker?

Where is the wind blowing from? How strong?

What shots are available to you? Can you play a fade or draw?

Are you "on" a club or between clubs?

Can you get backspin on the ball?

?

reversed if the trouble/flag is on the other side of the green.

Don't forget that you can place your ball close to the tee marker and stand outside the area if you wish. You can also take the ball back from between the markers (up to two club lengths).

The extra two or three yards might make it easier for you to select a club and perhaps play a full swing in your shot.

Finally make sure the teeing area and markers are aligned towards the green. Sometimes they are not and tend to "point" players in the wrong direction.

PRO TIP Don't go for every flag! Only go for the flag when it suits your eye – when you can visualize the shot and play it.

Tiger Woods hits from the left edge of the teeing area at the par three 12th hole at the Augusta National Golf Club. The shrubbery behind, traps, and water (plus a narrow, fast green) make this an intimidating hole, where good decision making is as crucial as excellent shotmaking.

Hitting the greens from the fairway Are you being too aggressive?

Hard lesson

A common mistake when hitting to a green either from the rough, fairway, or a tee (on a par 3) is being too aggressive. Going for a flag that is tucked away on a slope, or in a corner of a green, may be just too risky. You may find this a very hard lesson to absorb, but aiming directly at the flag will lead to more dropped shots than gained ones. Even top professionals will aim for the centre of the green if a flag is tucked away.

With hazards on the left and a large bunker to the right of the green Francesco Molinari doesn't have many options as he approaches the green. He was lucky that heavy rain had made the greens soft and holding so he could fire at the pin.

Within limits

The key is to play within your limits, so if you are a right-handed, natural fader of the ball then, when a flag is on the left side of the green, you should routinely aim to play safe. Conversely, flags located on the right side of the green will suit your eye better because you can aim at the middle of the green, allowing for the left-to-right fade to take the ball closer to the flag.

PRO TIP Don't forget to identify your target area. Don't be distracted and end up simply aiming at the pin.

Keep your head down!

With a tricky shot towards the green, there is a big temptation to raise the head. Keep looking down at the back of the ball and stay looking at it until you can see the ground/divot beneath where it was lying.

Hitting the greens from the fairway Check/understand the ball position

The position of the ball plays a big part in every shot a golfer makes, but when it comes to irons it's even more important. As you know, the ball position related to your stance depends on the club you are using. If you use long irons, the ball is normally forward in the stance; shorter clubs and you will have the ball towards the back. But why? Understanding this may help you focus more on the shot.

Shaft length and swing plane

The key reason for this is the length of shaft and how the swing plane changes.

The more loft a club has the shorter the shaft (a 9 iron is shorter than an 8 iron) and the shorter the shaft, the more you will have to bend over to create the correct posture. The more you have to bend, the steeper the swing naturally becomes, and the steeper the swing becomes the more you will have to move back to allow for the club to strike the ball correctly and impart the spin that is required by that certain club. A shorter club means more loft, more loft means more spin, and more spin means more control. The converse is, of course, true of longer clubs.

Checking ball position

So, when playing badly from the fairway, always take time to check the ball position. And remember that the ball position may change too if you don't have a flat lie.

This is the stance for a typical pitching wedge. This shot brings the posture into a more crouched position to compensate for the shorter length of shaft. The ball is slightly back from centre.

PRO TIP It's easy to focus on one aspect of your play – club selection, alignment, target area – and forget about others. Ball position can get overlooked so build it into a routine and check it before you play.

The classic mid-iron, mid-position stance. It is no coincidence that many teachers start novices off with a 7 iron. This is an excellent place from which to build and modify a swing.

Driving stance

Although this page is about fairway shots, it's good to remind yourself about stance when using the driver in contrast to mid- and short-iron shots. The posture here demonstrates a more upright stance (with the longer shaft) with the ball well forward, ideally just inside the left heel.

Hitting the greens from more than 150 yards Ball position and swing action

From distance you will be choosing longer clubs with less loft. The ball position will move further forward in the stance to allow for the shallower angle of attack, which will impart less spin and more distance. In this situation an incorrect ball position can be very costly.

Costly errors

If the ball is too far forwards you may strike the ground first and have a fat shot or – perhaps more commonly – strike the ball at the very start of your follow-through (on the upswing) and top it. A ball position too far back will nearly always result in a thinned shot, the blade cutting into the back of the ball. Both errors can be costly.

It's interesting to note that players can often self-correct these kind of faults by either leaning back or forward. This may bring short-term rewards, but result in a poor swing plane and probably loss of distance and accuracy.

Sweeping motion

Remember that for a long iron shot, the emphasis is more on a sweeping action rather than a downward strike into the ball. As explained elsewhere, this is because the shaft is longer in length and your posture is more upright, "taller", which creates a flatter swing and brings the club down into the ball on a shallower angle of attack. This gives a clean strike, with little or no divot, and creates the ideal long-iron shot.

Like everything in golf, you're looking for perfection! If the angle of attack becomes too shallow, which means the swing has become too flat, the result is likely to be a topped shot.

Preferred angle – although it will depend on club chosen.

Vertical

How NOT to do it

This pose highlights one of the common problems with fairway shots. The player is standing slightly too tall, probably because he is too close to the ball and is using a very flat backswing. The shot may well be topped and the swing restricted.

Ernie Els hits his second shot at the par 5, 3rd hole at the Dubai Desert Classic at the Emirates Golf Club. He has chosen a fairway wood to go for the green in two shots. His body has got through the ball really well and the club has brushed the ball off the surface taking no divot.

Hitting the greens from more than 150 yards Have a default sequence

When you're striking the ball well from the fairway the game seems quite simple. You're confident, hitting your targets, and scoring well. But, as you know, lots can go wrong. Poor long iron shots from the fairway are often the first thing to go astray and can have a serious effect on the rest of your game, notably your confidence.

Back-to-basics

A good plan is to have a back-to-basics swing sequence, a kind of default setting, that you can return to in order to produce a decent shot. This may mean playing within yourself and playing for safety, but hopefully it means you can get back on track and feel more confident that you can hit the shot you want.

Repeatable routine

One cure for mental and physical tension is the development of a repeatable routine. This might involve:
- visualising the shot by standing behind the ball;
- aiming, by placing the club behind the ball towards the intended target;

- checking the grip, set-up and alignment;
- releasing tension, such as by relaxing the forearms to avoid a too-tight grip.

Different players will develop slightly different routines, but consistence is both the key and the goal.

PRO TIP Nearly 90 per cent of all poor shots can be traced back to the set-up. This should be checked first before any swing alterations are considered.

The classic drive

You will know when a drive feels right and each part is in place. It may be helpful to break it down mentally, but ultimately it needs to be one smooth sequence with steady take back, a slight pause at the top of the backswing, and acceleration through the ball.

Hitting the greens from less than 150 yards Playing with short irons

Less than 150 yards and you'll be using the shorter irons: 7, 8, 9, and pitching wedge (PW). It's no coincidence that these are known as the "scoring clubs". They are so-called because more spin is generated by these clubs providing more control and a greater chance of accuracy.

When using the shorter clubs, the spin is greater due to the loft, and therefore the angle of attack becomes steeper.

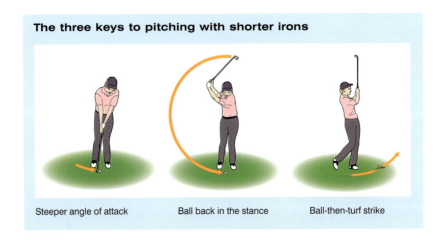

The three keys to pitching with shorter irons

Steeper angle of attack · Ball back in the stance · Ball-then-turf strike

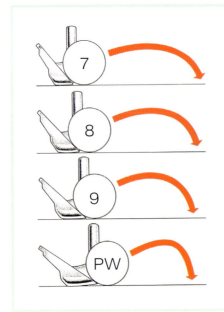

REMEMBER

Use this visual to keep clearly in your mind a set of distances for each of your short irons, from pitching wedge to 7 iron. These should be distances the balls can "carry", from you to where they land. You need to add on extra distance for roll, or subtract it if you can create backspin. When playing your shot you start with your distance and then alter yardages for the different conditions, for example in the weather or terrain.

After you've checked your alignment, don't forget to put the ball back in the stance. This ensures a ball-then-turf strike. Divots should be bigger and deeper when using the shorter irons. You should bring the club down steeply, but you must complete the follow-through. You are still swinging the club, not jabbing at the ball. The divot is the result of a good shot, not an aim in itself.

PRO TIP When using short irons you want to get the feeling of really hitting *down* into the *back* of the ball.

Lee Westwood of England plays his approach shot on the 18th hole at the Laguna National Golf Club in Singapore. The divot shows how he has hit down. Note also his head; there is little chance of his looking up and topping his shot.

Hitting the greens from less than 150 yards Coping with difficult lies

Difficult lies don't only occur when you're less than 150 yards from the green, but here is a good place to remind yourself of the basics – and to rectify what might be going wrong.

Ball below the feet

If the ball is below your feet, your posture will be more bent over which will automatically create a much steeper swing and angle of attack. This will affect the flight in three ways:

- the ball will tend to fly higher;
- there will be more spin (both due to steeper angle);
- the ball is likely to spin to the right (the steeper swing also produces more of an out-to-in swing path).

Be aware of these factors and adjust your set-up accordingly.

Ball above your feet

Much of the above is reversed when you have the ball above your feet. The swing becomes much flatter due to the slope and creates a more in-to-out swing path tending to hook the ball off left of centre (for a right-hander). Also the ball will fly lower due to the flatter angle of attack.

Working with the slope

In both instances, work with the slope. The more severe the slope the more you must adjust, but you must always try to make your spine perpendicular to the slope. The more severe the slope the more severe the reaction the ball will have to that.

PRO TIP Don't focus overly on the slope issues and forget other basics.

Playing the ball off a slope

A clear reminder of the likely effect of playing the ball off a slope. Allow for the slope but also make sure you hit through the ball, with the follow-through aiming at your target, and focus keenly on the ball. There is a danger of topping shots when the ball is beneath your feet.

In this shot the ball will be above your feet with the danger of playing a hooked shot. With this situation you need to be careful not to hit the ball fat. Take extra practice swings on similarly sloping ground before hitting your shot.

REMEMBER A downslope reduces the effective loft of your club. For example, a 7 iron may behave like a 5 iron with lower loft and more run. Greater distance is the likely result of a well-struck downhill lie.

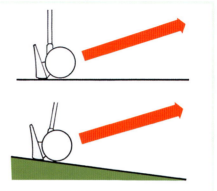

Uphill and downhill lies

Although different from above and below your feet, it is worth reminding yourself of the "rules" relating to uphill and downhill lies.

Downhill lie

- spine perpendicular to slope with shoulders forward;
- solid footing to avoid loss of balance and falling forward;
- altered club selection – maybe choosing one or two clubs less.

Uphill lie

- spine perpendicular to slope with shoulders tilted back;
- solid footing to avoid loss of balance and falling backwards;
- altered club selection – maybe choosing one or two clubs more.

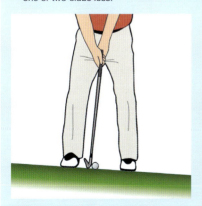

Downhill lie – put the ball back in your stance.

Uphill lie – put the ball forward in your stance.

Missing greens from the
fairway Alignment masterclass

It's been said before, but the first thing you should check if there is a directional problem is alignment. It cannot be stressed enough how important it is. No refinements or enhancements of a swing should be considered until your alignment has been checked. This is something even the top pros work on continuously. If your alignment is incorrect, the intended target will hardly ever be found, no matter how good your swing is.

Take help where you can

When practising alignment always place clubs on the ground to assist you and, at every possible opportunity, ask a friend to stand behind you and check your knees, hips, and shoulders (see pages 138–139). During a social or practice

The player demonstrates simple off-course exercises to ensure correct alignment. The four areas are feet, knees, hips/waist, and shoulders.

round you can ask your playing partner to look at your alignment. Some driving ranges have mirrors, too. The golf swing is hard enough, so it's important to get the static element right first – this is the easy part. Check it and doublecheck it.

What can go wrong?

If it is easy, how can alignment let you down? The most common reason is that you set up correctly and then, at the last minute, decide to change one element. Most commonly you might think you're

not aiming in the right direction and subtly move your feet – forgetting to shift everything else, too. Or you might mentally have a different shape of shot in your mind than the one you're set for and minutely shift your hands relative to the ball – but nothing else.

If you are not happy with your set-up, don't just move one element, start again, getting everything into alignment.

Ernie Els chipping on the practice ground with his coach. A pair of eyes watching from behind will help iron out alignment problems.

PRO TIP You're warned against slow play, but a few extra seconds taken on checking alignment will always be worth it.

Still missing greens from the fairway Grip masterclass

Apart from alignment, the other main reasons for missing too many greens from the fairway are the old favourites of grip and swing plane. Grip is, arguably, the most important part of the set-up.

Aligning V-shapes

As before, if the grip is producing too much right-to-left spin then you tend to be showing too many knuckles in the left hand (for a right-handed golfer). Either this, or the V-shapes created between the thumbs and forefingers are pointing too far right of the player's right shoulder.

Start with the palms

One problem that can easily be rectified is the way the palms are positioned when taking your grip on the club. To start with, the palms should naturally face one another.

During the swing and then at impact, your palms still return to the position they naturally want to be in – facing each other. If your hands are too much one way or the other – too much to the left (weak) or too much to the right (strong) – then they will probably be so at impact, thus either closing or opening the clubface.

It's only a glove!

Your choice of glove is important. Ideally choose one that is medium to tight fit. A loose, or overly tight, glove will not allow you the correct contact you require. Many players like to use a glove for drives and long iron shots, but take it off for round-the-green shots and for putting. They like to have greater "feel" for these more delicate shots. It is advised to have a consistent policy for these shots. A wet glove can be useless; carry several in your bag for rainy days, or don't use one at all.

REMEMBER

The most important thing is to have the hands correctly positioned on the club. However, the grip itself can be altered, being made thinner or thicker by adding or removing layers of tape. It's highly recommended to have this done professionally.

Facing palms together is a very good way of starting out your set-up. When working on the grip, any change to your existing set-up may, at first, feel peculiar. It is worth persevering so that the changed (and correct) grip soon becomes natural and an integral part of your play.

PRO TIP Check your grip at address to ensure you are holding the club in the fingers and *not* the palm, as a palm grip will restrict the wrist action.

Still missing greens from the fairway Swing plane masterclass

Your club's shaft position at the top of the backswing is crucial. It could be pointing right or left of target, encouraging an in-to-out or out-to-in swing path.

Shaft position

Check the shaft position at waist height during a practice swing. Make sure that the shaft is pointing along a parallel line to your feet and body. If this position is correct then it becomes much easier to achieve the correct position at the top of the backswing.

Swing in sections

There is nothing wrong with mentally or physically breaking your swing into sections, checking correct alignment in each. By doing this you will tend to take back more slowly, and more correctly. Some players hold their club at the top of the backswing before beginning the swing sequence. This is fine providing you use the opportunity to ensure correct alignment before completing the swing.

These photos show a take-away that is too "inside" (1) at the top of the backswing where the club is pointing right of target (2). This will cause the ball to start right of target.

PRO TIP If the ball spins to the right of target then clubface is the fault; if it starts right of target then swing or alignment needs attention.

The swing in four parts: take-away (1), top of backswing (2), downswing (3), and follow-through (4). Try looking at each part separately in your practice sessions.

Still missing greens from the fairway The lie of your clubface

Too upright?

A big factor in the ball flight when using an iron is the lie. If the lie of an iron is too upright this means that, at impact, the heel of the club is digging into the ground and the toe is in the air. The effect of this is to twist the club at impact and cause it to close, creating right to left spin. This will also tend to make the ball come off the face nearer to the toe, which will result in loss of power.

...or too flat?

The opposite is true if the lie of the club is too flat. An iron that is too flat means that, at impact, the toe of the club is

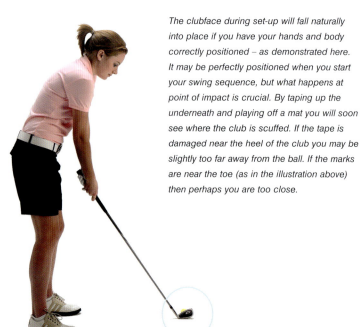

The clubface during set-up will fall naturally into place if you have your hands and body correctly positioned – as demonstrated here. It may be perfectly positioned when you start your swing sequence, but what happens at point of impact is crucial. By taping up the underneath and playing off a mat you will soon see where the club is scuffed. If the tape is damaged near the heel of the club you may be slightly too far away from the ball. If the marks are near the toe (as in the illustration above) then perhaps you are too close.

striking the ground and the heel is raised. In this case the club will twist open and create left to right spin. Loss of power will also be noticed – it will feel like the ball is struck nearer the heel of the club.

You can check the lie yourself by placing tape on the sole of an iron, then hitting some iron shots. If the tape is wearing towards the toe area, your clubs could be too flat, vice versa if the tape is wearing towards the heel.

PRO TIP If you notice a problem and can't easily rectify it, your clubs may be too long or short. Go to your local golf professional and ask about a fitting.

The taped club
While on the subject of strike you can also use the taped club to see where you are striking the ball on the face of the club. Near the toe may mean hooked shots; the heel could induce a sliced shot.

REMEMBER
A round-soled club might prove easier to hit than a flat-soled club, especially on uneven fairways. The current trend of using hybrid (wood/iron mix) clubs often gives players greater confidence, but you need to check the sole of these clubs – they are often quite flat – to make sure they suit you.

Problems from inside 100 yards Judgment, practice, and strategy

Once your distance to the green becomes less than 100 yards the shot turns into a matter of judgment rather than just picking the right club. Most amateur golfers will admit to practising about 25 per cent short game and 75 per cent long game; top pros are more likely to have the 25/75 split the other way round. It's no coincidence that a top pro could probably play a 90-yard shot with any club just because their feel and judgment is so good through all the practice.

You need to work on judgment – but not only of distance but also type of shot. What shots can you play? Is a bump and

Decisions, decisions. Australia's Adam Scott consults his caddie prior to taking a fairway shot during the fourth round of the $2.3m Johnnie Walker Classic in Beijing. Top players take a lot of time in thinking and consulting.

run, perhaps played with a 7 or 8 iron, a good option or are you floating the ball up on to the green?

Is there an obstruction in your way (a bunker or section of rough) and do you have much green to play with when it lands? Is the trouble at the back or front, are the greens holding the ball, what's your lie like? Perhaps your problem with hitting good shots from 100 yards is not just about touch and practice but also about having the right strategy. What's the answer?

- assess the options you have from 100 yards;
- work hard on these in practice so you develop good judgment of distance;
- work out a clear strategy when faced with a shot – the more options you have, the easier this will be;
- stick to the strategy and play the shot accordingly.

Of course you will have a favourite shot, the floated wedge, the pitch and run, the flat 8 iron, and you will favour this, but the more options you have, the better your score will be.

PRO TIP For distances of 100 yards, 75 yards, and 50 yards, shots need to be judged by the length of the backswing. Practise hitting 100-yard shots with a full swing, then with the same club 75-yard shots and then 50-yard shots. This will teach your body the feeling of different distances, something that is essential for wedge play.

The target area

The target area is defined by the shot you can play. Although the flighted shot (C), played with backspin, might be ideal, a hard lie might dissuade you from the shot; you might not feel confident in playing it. The flatter chip (B) might be playable, but it means hitting closer to the trap and relying upon the roll of the ball once it hits the green. Though the cautious shot (A) may minimize birdie chances, it could be the best option in the long run.

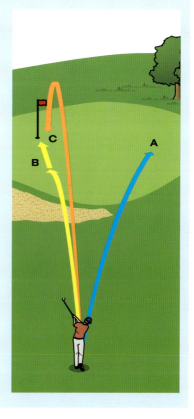

Problems from inside 100 yards Ball position and wrist action

If you are pitching into the green and having mixed success you should check both ball position and wrist action. The ball position must be far enough back in the stance to ensure that the club is striking down into the back of the ball creating enough spin.

The spin on the ball is important because, as the club isn't travelling as fast as a full swing, the spin isn't automatically created. By placing the ball slightly further back than normal this will ensure the club will strike the ball first, thus increasing the spin rate.

For top scoring from close in, spin is so important. The more spin you can create, the more control you have on the ball; the more control you have, the more likely you are to get closer to the flag. The result: more one putts, better overall scores. Choose the strategy you feel most confident with but for really good scoring you need to develop excellent control.

The photographs demonstrate two problems with short, wristy shots. Left, the ball is well placed, but the player's wrists are not cocked enough and the swing could be too flat. Right, the player has well-cocked wrists and an ideal three-quarter backswing. Unfortunately the ball is too far forward in her stance.

Ball position is only part of the story. When playing a delicate shot you must be careful with the amount of wrist action you use.

What can happen is that, even though your swing tends to be slightly shorter than a full swing (depending on your strength and the distance of the shot), your hand speed can still be that of a full swing. This results in the hands un-cocking too soon and either a heavy, or a hooked shot, can be produced.

This is all to do with the feel and timing of your golf shots and where practice really does make perfect, or at least improvement!

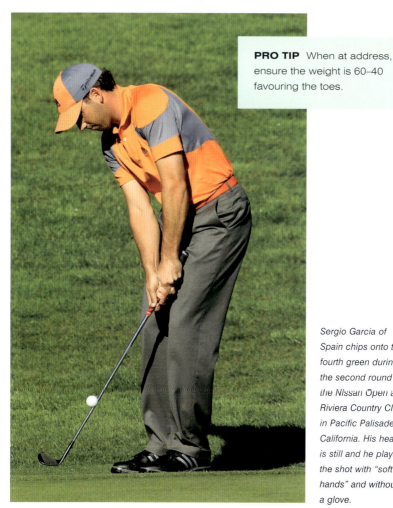

PRO TIP When at address, ensure the weight is 60–40 favouring the toes.

Sergio Garcia of Spain chips onto the fourth green during the second round of the Nissan Open at Riviera Country Club in Pacific Palisades, California. His head is still and he plays the shot with "soft hands" and without a glove.

Problems from inside 100 yards Hitting fat – hitting thin

These two problems affect many amateur players. There is nothing more frustrating than getting yourself in a good position and then spoiling it by poor contact on what will be a "touch" shot.

Swing thoughts

You've chosen your strategy, you are aligned, and the ball is positioned appropriately; what now goes through your mind?

- my shot is 80 yards;
- my pitching wedge goes 100 yards at full swing;
- I need to take 20 yards off my full wedge (there is no wind!);
- that's 20 per cent less power.

OK, so make practice swings trying to feel that 20 per cent going from your main swing – throughout the swing. Restrict the hand action slightly; keep it in step with the length and power of the swing. It is when only part of the swing operates at 20 per cent that the problems start.

Another reason for fat and thin shots can be to do with balance. Above (left), the player first leans too far over the ball (common in short pitch shots) and then (right) sits back on the shot (common where players are aiming for distance).

Setting goals

Importantly you should remember that players at different levels will have different expectations when it comes to pitching and the short game. You must be realistic about what you can expect. A low single-figure golfer will be looking to get more spin, control, and to get nearer the flag than a 15-handicap player who does have more shots to play with and is probably more satisfied with just hitting the green. It's all part of getting the balance right between technique, practice, expectations, and satisfaction.

REMEMBER

A classic beginner's error is to try to "lift" the ball in the swing. You must, of course, rely upon the shape of the clubhead to achieve loft in the shot. The club will do this. Any attempt to bring the ball up will usually result in a topped shot. Ironically the result will be that the ball is forced down by topspin.

PRO TIP When playing a shot of this type, a player must make more practice swings than normal; the emphasis is more on feel and judgment rather than club selection.

The classically balanced posture with the pressure just slightly on the front of the foot – just enough to support the lean over the ball.

Problems from inside 50 yards
Assess your lie and choose your shot

Any shot less than 50 yards is going to be 100 per cent feel and, although feel is something that cannot be taught (although it can be "learned"), there are common mistakes many players make.

PRO TIP If you have a difficult lie think carefully about the shot. Don't be rushed and then find you are in equal trouble after the shot.

Check the lie
The first thing you should do before playing any type of shot, and especially those close in, is assess the lie.

If the ball is sitting high on a fluffy piece of grass then you would approach it differently than if it were on a patch of bone dry soil or on a replaced divot. The better the lie the more control you can get because more spin is produced off shorter, tighter grass.

Assuming the lie is good you may want to opt for a pitch or lob shot (be sure you understand the difference between the two). Double-check you have the correct ball position; any pitch shot from less that 50 yards needs to have the ball right back towards the right toe to ensure as much spin as possible. If you want to play a lob shot however, the ball position will be further forward,

Good lie
You have a good lie – you therefore have choices about what shot to play. Think now about what shot you feel most confident about and what approach the hole requires.

First cut
The ball is in the first cut so presents few problems but remember to pick the ball off the grass; there is a danger of playing under the ball and flying it only a few feet (see also page 200).

nearer the inside of the left heel. This will allow the club to slide under the ball more, creating the extra loft.

Different approach
When the lie is poor then a different approach must be taken. A poor lie almost certainly means less spin will be produced so you must allow for more roll.

When picturing the shot, you need to imagine where to land the ball and then how much the ball will roll. Practising from both rough and fairway will help you to learn how a ball reacts from a good and poor lie.

A bizarre lie? The key is to minimize the damage. What are the dangers if you miscue? Can you get out with a shot – or is a drop a better option?

Tight lie
A hard lie, maybe on baked mud or some other surface. First check whether you can get relief from a path or GUR. If not, remember the club will probably "bounce" off the surface so there is a greater danger of thinning the ball. A flat chip and run might be better than an ambitious chip.

Uneven lie
A sloping lie with the ball in a small hollow. Think carefully about how you will hit this shot. There are many factors to take into consideration (club, stance, target area) but once you've decided what you are going to do, commit to the shot and don't decelerate in the downswing.

Ball on divot
The ball sits on a replaced divot – one of the most dangerous lies you can have as the ground will move under your club, moving your ball, too. Try to engineer a shot that allows you to pick the ball first, having the ball back in the stance to achieve this.

Problems from inside 50 yards
Are you using the right ball for your game?

A question of feel

Feel is a part of the short game that cannot be stressed enough. If you cannot "feel" a shot, it then becomes guesswork, and when you guess at something it normally doesn't turn out for the best. This is why the type of ball you use has an effect on pitching.

Low handicap players tend to use the softer feeling balls, that is a ball with a softer cover. These provide a higher spin rate – thus more control. Players talk of extra feel with "soft" balls.

Touch or distance

Golfers who use balls with a harder cover will find that when they chip or pitch, and even putt, the ball will feel hard off the clubface and will roll a lot more. This, of course, can be fine for driving longer distances if that's what you require. However when you face a shot that requires some stop on the ball then the options are limited.

You need to have confidence in every aspect of your game and equipment (see also pages 210–211) including the ball.

It's only the ball!

Just as with the glove (see page 168) the choice of ball is important. Though it is a good idea to have one type of ball that you can use most of the time, you will want to change from time to time, perhaps for different courses and probably for different seasons. If possible, fill your practice bag (shagbag) with the same kind of ball that you use during play on the course.

PRO TIP One word: *practice*! The more time you spend on the practice green the better your feel will become.

If the first word is "practice", the second is probably "confidence". Practice is something you can do, but confidence is an intangible and fragile part of your game that can come and go. Most professionals, many of whom use sports psychologists to help them, aim to believe they are going to win the competitions they enter, although, of course, they rarely do. This shot from Ai Miyazato of Japan exudes great confidence, in addition to good technique.

Problems from inside 50 yards
Be clear with your strategy to avoid heavy shots

Your feel only improves with practice. Though a professional shouldn't admit this, chipping, pitching, and putting will all improve even with a poor technique if you practise.

Taking the lessons learned on the practice ground onto the course is a different matter. You may find that what went well in practice doesn't work on the course. One reason is that you are failing to stick to your plan – failing to commit to the shot.

Don't quit on the shot
Heavy shots – where you hit the ground before the ball – is a typical problem and can occur for a number of reasons. Just because you have a reduced backswing you shouldn't un-cock the wrists too soon. Un-cocking early will give an "early hit".

Similarly your reduced swing doesn't mean reduced speed. A slow or "floppy" swing will mean early hitting – bringing the clubface down too early or too soon. This tends to be a mistake made by golfers with slower swings. In both cases, stick to the shot, use a reduced swing, but keep up the sequence and the rhythm.

Forearm/wrist angle
A good way to stop heavy or early hitting is, while practising, trying to hold the angle between the left forearm and the club shaft at 90°. Wait until the club gets parallel to the ground then un-cock the wrists and release that angle.

The timing of this is difficult, but if successful, will create a much stronger strike and increased power. The technique obviously gives you less time to actually get the clubface square to the ball, so initially the strike should improve, but the ball can possibly shoot off to the right. This is due to the clubface still being open. Your hands will have to learn to rotate faster to ensure a square clubface at impact. It's another case of practice being required to improve technique and take shots off your game.

Scuffing the ground
The dreaded heavy or fat shot where the ground-then-ball strike normally leads to loss of distance. With hard ground and a highly angled club you may also "bounce" the club and thin the shot. Apart from poor technique in the strike (see opposite) the most common reason for this is loss of acceleration on the downswing. The answer is to commit – don't quit – on the shot.

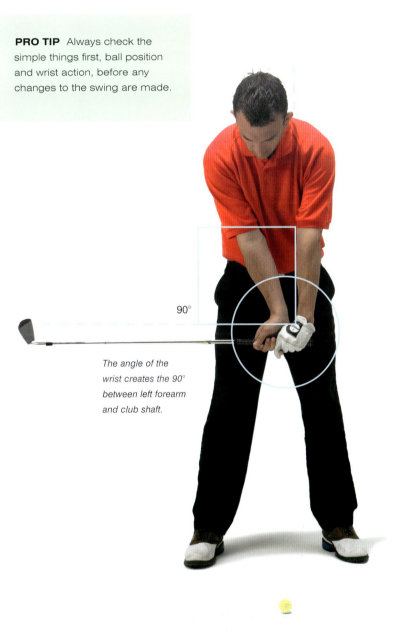

Fault fixer:
Improve your game

PRO TIP Always check the simple things first, ball position and wrist action, before any changes to the swing are made.

90°

The angle of the wrist creates the 90° between left forearm and club shaft.

Checking the correct angle between left forearm and shaft. The shot will then be a smooth but accelerating punch into the back of the ball.

Problems from inside 50 yards   185

In a fairway bunker Get as much distance as you can

Most amateur players are disappointed, and a little anxious, when they hit into the bunkers. Greenside bunkers require touch and technique, but are fairway bunkers a different proposition?

Thought and technique

Dealing with the ball in a fairway trap requires both careful thought and good technique but, unlike the greenside bunker, there may be a bit more room for error. First you will need to decide your goals – length and direction – but these will be determined by the lie of the ball and the height of the bunker wall in front of you. Assuming you have a good lie and the wall in front of you is not too steep, think carefully about what club you can play, or need to play.

Don't forget, you can use anything from a fairway trap from a low-angled hybrid to a 60° wedge; your distance can be anything from 200-plus yards to just a few feet. Another important tip is

to grip the club fractionally lower than for the equivalent fairway shot. This will help make a clearer, "thinner" shot.

Putting safety first

Importantly, make sure you get out of the sand and that your next shot is from the fairway (or green). Don't hit from one hazard into another!

You may have many swing thoughts in your mind when you are standing over the ball in a fairway bunker. Try to simplify it.

- Are you happy with your club? If not go back and think again.
- Are you happy with the shot you want to play? If not, get out of the trap and take another practice swing.
- Are you focused on your goal? If not, think again before playing your shot.

A fairway bunker can add one shot to your score, but it doesn't have to. Most crucial of all, a fairway bunker should not add more than one shot to your score.

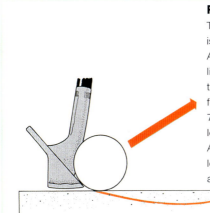

REMEMBER

The amount of sand you take is crucial to a shot from a trap. Assuming you have fairly standard, light sand then you may want to take just a small amount of sand for shots from between 25 and 75 yards (see above). Anything longer and you want a clean strike. Anything shorter and you are looking at more sand and possibly a "splash" shot.

Vijay Singh (left) playing from distance from a trap at the TPC Boston. The fact that he has taken a small amount of sand suggests that he has chosen a high-angled club, perhaps a wedge. As a big hitter he can afford to do this. From distance you may have to play a "thinner" shot, picking the ball off the top, to reach your goal. Always check the height of the face in front of you before making your club choice. Will you make the height safely?

PRO TIP Make sure you know all the rules about playing in the trap – can you remove stones? what if your ball is leaning against the rake? – so that you have to focus only on your shot.

In a greenside bunker Taking too much, or too little, sand

Assessing depth of sand

The biggest problem with bunker shots is taking the right amount of sand and that's why the set-up is so important. The first thing you should do when entering a bunker is shuffle your feet in the sand to try to gauge its depth and texture. This is not for show – this will make a difference to your shot.

Once this has been defined then you can decide how much sand needs to be taken to produce the distance required. Also, setting your feet into the sand allows for a good grounding, but do remember that if you sink into the sand by an inch or two then your grip may need to be down the shaft by the same amount.

The main reason for taking too much sand is if the clubface enters the sand too square. In this case the leading edge will actually strike the sand. The leading edge is much sharper than the sole of the club so this would cause the club to cut into the sand. This generally happens due to incorrect hand action. If the hand action is too active, this will

PRO TIP Hone your technique so you get out every time. Work on varying distances only when you are confident of the basics.

cause the club to close and make the leading edge to enter the sand rather than the sole.

Clear objective

Of course, the whole purpose of a bunker shot is to actually strike the sand and not the ball, so hitting the ball too early will mean less sand and a strike that is too clean. Normally the cause of this is that the ball is too far back in the stance.

So, feet in the sand, ball not too far back, and a sound swing keeping the club at the correct angle and taking the right amount of sand. Easy, but it isn't always the case, so look at pages 190–191 for more help.

Finally, check the sand for consistency and water content. A more positive swing will be required in wet sand.

Sand wedge

The shape of a sand wedge is designed to allow you to play into the sand. The flat sole of the club resists the sand and bounces out and up as you carry your swing forward. Play a normal swing and don't try to scoop the ball out; the club will do the business.

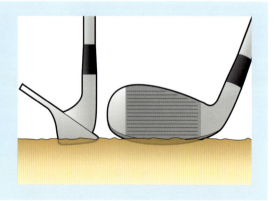

Tiger Woods hits his second shot out of a greenside bunker on the 10th hole at Royal Liverpool
Golf Club in Hoylake, England. British and European links courses typically have these steep-
sided traps where, sometimes, it is necessary to play out sideways. The key is to get out first time,
every time – or not go into them in the first place!

In a greenside bunker
Taking away the fear factor

Top professionals don't worry unduly about being in a trap – they know they can get out and, usually, put the ball where they want it. You may be different. One of the problems of bunker play is that a different mindset takes over and players are more anxious about the shot.

Back to basics

The key to taking away the fear is to remember your first bunker lessons, go back to the classic shot, and play with confidence. Remind yourself of the key points:

- set the body in a position to encourage the swing to be on a plane that will create the right angle of attack – one that is more likely to strike the sand before the ball;
- ensure your feet, knees, hips, and shoulders are pointing left of target – how much left of target depends on the length of shot and depth of sand;
- concentrate on keeping the clubface pointing at the target at address;
- keep the clubface open during the swing path and at impact, otherwise the ball will travel in the direction of the swing path that is left of target.

Angle of attack

Why are these "rules" so vital? With the body pointing left of target you are creating an out-to-in swing path, which produces a steeper angle of attack. It's this that ensures the club strikes the sand before the ball.

By keeping the clubface open during impact you ensure the loft stays constant and, most importantly, guarantee that the sole of the club strikes the sand causing the club to bounce out of the sand rather than digging in. When playing a bunker shot you shouldn't feel the ball on the face of your club, only sand.

Because of the cushioning effect of the sand you need to take a more expansive swing than for a chip shot of the same distance. The key is to let the sand slow the ball. Never die on a bunker shot; you will find yourself with another bunker shot!

Remember the basics. Play with confidence. If you stand square to the target and use conventional hand action you will find a lot of shots very hard to control as you are much more likely to strike the ball first.

Trust technique
The angle of attack to the ball: Your alignment, and swing plane, is a little left of target while the open face points at the target. The ball will fly straight.

PRO TIP Shuffling feet into the sand will lower the body, giving the player more chance of striking the sand.

The greenside trap shot that gently lifts the ball up over a steep bunker wall and onto the green is often called the "splash" shot. Paula Creamer of the United States demonstrates this. You can clearly see the sand she has taken and the open clubface.

Too many putts Sorting out your distances

Speed control

The key to putting is distance control. Distance control, or speed, is the first thing you should be thinking about over any length of putt, especially the longer putts. When you go to the practice putting green before teeing off (and you should *always* go to the practice putting green before teeing off) the only thing on your mind should be speed.

Consistency of greens

Spend time hitting different lengths of putts and just concentrate on getting the speed correct. The more putts you hit, the easier it is to judge the pace. This will make a huge difference once you are on the course. If you have time visit one or two greens on the course and look at them. Check that the practice green is similar; it should be.

During the round you will face putts of varying distance so make sure your practice includes everything from 4 feet to 40 feet. To gain a feel for speed, putt on the same stretch of green, ideally with no slope.

One to get close, and one for the hole

Balls laid out from one side of the hole are good for practising either uphill or downhill putts. You get into the groove quickly. Importantly vary your practice, use your normal technique, and remember that sometimes a two-putt will do. Aggressively trying to sink every shot can lead to problems on fast sloping greens.

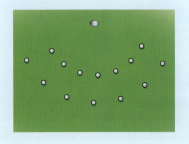

REMEMBER

It is worth understanding the physics of putting. The ball will begin with a slide over the first ball length or two. Then it develops into a forward, base over apex, roll. Finally, in the last moments before inertia it may wobble into a settled position. Hit your putt firmly enough to get it to the hole before it wobbles.

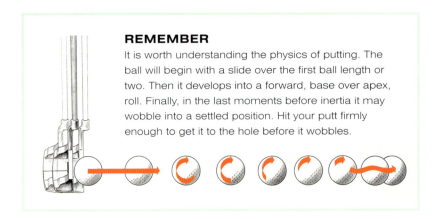

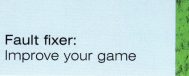

PRO TIP The key to getting putts to roll better is to slightly strike them on the upswing; this puts less spin on and gets the balls hugging the ground sooner.

*Try to simulate match conditions by practising with your normal routine –
perhaps using marks on the ball to show the line, removing the flagstick,
and putting without a glove.*

Too many putts Develop a regime for reading the lie

Although the pace is the first issue, reading the breaks of a green is also key. You will have your own technique, but is it working for you? Good reading of heavily sloped greens will definitely save you shots.

Start from the lowest point

The best place to spot slope is from the lowest part of the green. First, look for high and low areas. This will give you an overall indication of the line of the putt. It is unlikely that putts will not follow the general slope. Then you're looking for the subtle slopes that are harder to find. Don't be lazy, always kneel down so your eye line is nearer the ground. Try to look at the line between your ball and the hole from the same distance each time – say 5 feet behind the ball. This will give your reading greater consistency.

Use the time well

Use your time around the green well, looking at the green as you approach it and as you walk around it to put your bag down. Keep thinking while your opponents or partners are playing and always try to learn from their putts.

Even if you know your own course well, don't slack in your regime. Go through the same processes each time and these will help you when you visit unfamiliar surroundings.

PRO TIP The quicker the putt, the more break it will have.

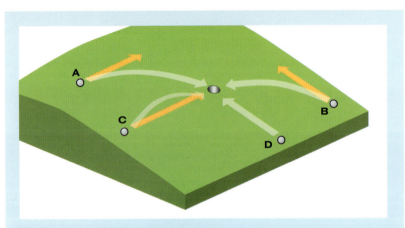

Playing across the slope

Playing across the slope (as in A, B, and C) is the hardest putt to make. The yellow arrows show the plane of the green, the white show the likely shape of shot. In cases like these it is advisable to use enough pace to get the ball up to the hole and not much more. In D, a relatively straightforward shot directly uphill, you can afford to hit firmly at the back of the cup, taking away any likelihood of unexpected break.

Don't cut corners in practice

This routine is a simple reminder to hit from different distances and directions in practice. If you do miss (as in the third photo) walk up and tap it in. Very short putts need practice, too. Give yourself goals that you must achieve before you walk off the green.

Missed putts from 10 feet
Thinking about alignment, pace, and lie

Setting targets

You probably don't expect to hole all, or even many, of your "ten footers" but it would be good to see some of them going in. The first key, therefore, is to set your target and measure yourself against this. Say, on average, you get 9 putts sitting between 5 and 20 feet in a round. Perhaps your target should be to sink two of them, but never to get down in more than two from that distance.

The 10-foot range is a difficult distance because your brain is telling you that you should have a good chance of holing it but, depending on the actual putt, this may not be the case. For example, if a putt is 10 feet slightly uphill with no break this will be much easier than a 10-foot putt, sharply downhill, with a 2-foot break.

If you're having difficulty from this distance, think about your options. The facts are the more break in a putt, the harder it is to read. The quicker the greens the harder to gauge the speed. And the quicker the greens the more a putt will break.

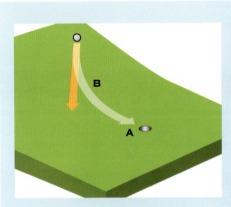

Downhill putts

With this downhill putt you may see the shape of the putt curving down into the hole (B), but don't be tempted to align yourself at the cup (A). Set yourself up to play the ball in the direction you are going to strike it.

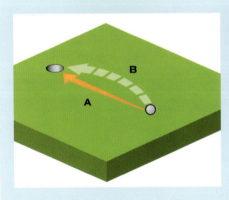

Playing the break

Remember – it's either a firm putt straight (A) at the back of the cup or a gentle one to take the borrow (B). Decide your policy and carry it through. Don't mix and match!

Visualizing the shot

So, with this information, you have to first of all imagine how you wish to see the ball getting to the hole, at a firm pace or just dropping in dead. Your decision affects the amount of break you allow for the putt.

Hitting the putts at different speeds has both positive and negative sides. The positives of hitting a putt firmer are that it will have less break, so is easier to read, and being firm with a stroke builds confidence. The downside of hitting the putt firm is that if you miss it, the next putt back will be much longer than if you hit it dead weight.

The key is to build a general policy, what you prefer to do in your game as a whole, then try to follow it. Sometimes, however, you will choose the other option. That's fine, but once you make a decision, *stick to it*. A mis-match – for example, allowing for break, then putting fast – will end in disappointment.

PRO TIP The putting green is the best place to improve. Practising uphill, downhill, and sidehill putts will train your brain to read the greens better.

Annika Sorenstam of Sweden lines up her putt. A one-inch tap-in from a missed putt counts the same score as a 250-yard drive. Take time.

Missed putts from 3 feet
Monitor your grip for extra control

Sinking putts – building confidence

There is nothing worse than missing short putts and the problem is your brain doesn't let you forget that either. The answer is to build a stroke that is repetitive, so eventually the short putts become straightforward.

The grip plays a part in all areas of the game but, when putting, the stroke is much slower than a full swing, so it has more chance of moving the clubface. There are many different types of grip that can be used as long as it does one thing – keep the clubface square at impact. Whether you are using a standard reverse overlap, or even a left-hand low grip, make sure that both thumbs are on the front of the grip, not slightly to the side as in the conventional "full swing" grip.

Minimize the movement

By keeping the thumbs down the centre of the grip and remaining there during the stroke, the clubface has less chance

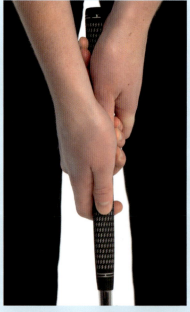

Classic grip (overlapping)
A classic grip for a standard putter. Putters normally have squared-off grips, which make aligning the thumbs down the shaft more natural.

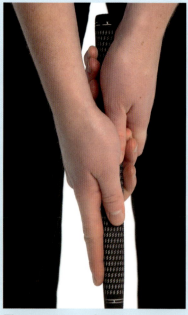

Finger steer grip
This is not everybody's favourite grip, but the finger along the back of the club provides a feeling of greater control and better "steering".

of twisting. If the club moves during the shot it's because you moved it. An optional extra, shown in the illustration, is to use the index finger for extra control. The choice is completely up to you, of course, but don't be distracted from the basic idea.

Use alignment aids

Perfecting the grip is part of the alignment process. Nearly all modern putters have a line, lines, or even circles to indicate alignment. They are there for a reason and you should use them to your advantage. Remind yourself of the imaginary line going through to the target and back behind the ball. Visualize this, keep the clubface square at impact and the ball will travel along that line.

Putting aids are also very useful to help with this alignment process; top players will always have a piece of string, a straight edge, or even a chalk line to help with the alignment and stroke for short putts.

Using the club's own features such as "balls" or lines of course helps. If, however, you still feel you are not hitting square-on you can use the tried and trusted method of putting between two tees. All your careful assessment of the green and lining up of the ball will be wasted if you don't hit the ball square on.

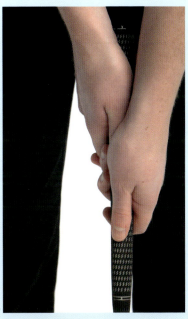

Reversed grip

Some left-handed people play golf right-handed and then choose this grip for putting. Experiment – it may suit you. Reversing your grip certainly refreshes your focus on the shot.

PRO TIP When practising, get a straight edge and get used to just putting along this straight edge; this will improve the stroke.

Leaving putts short Check your clubhead speed

Acceleration is the key

You can leave putts short for a number of reasons, but the most common is deceleration in the stroke. A putting stroke, like any other swing or stroke, needs to be attacking or accelerating through impact. Any deceleration in a stroke means that the clubface is actually slowing down as it strikes the ball causing it not to travel the distance you require.

Apart from practice there is little you can do to ensure you don't falter on the shot except, perhaps, have a swing thought. If you imagine that you had to drive a car through a brick wall you would accelerate through the wall, not brake!

Remember always that the key is accelerating. Don't be tempted to take a bigger backswing to counterbalance your deceleration. This might mean that, occasionally, the stroke will come through at the correct pace but normally the longer backswing just results in the ball going too far and out of control.

PRO TIP The follow-through on a short putt should be longer than the backswing; this will encourage an acceleration in the stroke.

Too much backswing

More backswing than follow-through is a recipe for a jabbed putt. Greater movement behind the ball increases the danger of misalignment and incorrect clubhead speed.

Good follow-through

A shorter backswing and longer follow-through create better control of the ball in both speed and direction. Practise this until it becomes second nature. You don't want too many swing thoughts while putting.

REMEMBER

Two extra practice routines for pace and accuracy. Either aim through tees or, for firm putts, try to target a tee placed at the back of the hole.

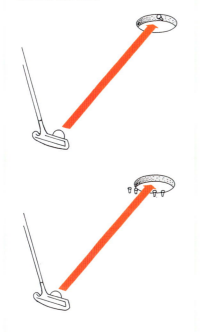

A good follow-through. Notice also that, although the ball is well on the way towards the hole, the player hasn't yet raised her head. Keep your head down. Some professionals recommend a practice routine where you can't look up until you hear the ball fall into the cup!

REMEMBER

To encourage a good follow-through you can push the ball along towards the hole from about 18 inches. Only try this in practice as a means to encourage forward movement. It is illegal in the game, of course.

Playing poorly from the rough
Thinking about your goals and planning your shot

As well as the occasional great shot, there are usually two results when playing from the rough – a flyer, or a wayward shot because of the club twisting.

Assess the possibilities

The first thing you should do when approaching any shot is to assess the lie. Don't begin to think about final targets until you have seen what is possible. The lie will have a huge impact on what the ball does.

A flying lie is generally where the rough isn't very thick and you can get at the ball relatively cleanly. A flying lie also implies, however, that the grass can get trapped in between the clubface and ball at impact. The result of this is normally very little spin and the ball rolling on further than planned. The only way to adapt to this lie is to take less club and allow for the extra distance, but remember when the ball lands it is likely to roll more as it has less backspin.

When the rough is thicker, flyers are less common but because the rough is thicker, the ball tends to sit down more. When a ball is sitting down in thicker rough you have the option of just taking a very lofted club and getting the ball back into play or taking a slight risk with a less lofted club in trying to advance the ball further.

What is your next shot?

Think carefully about the next shot after the rough shot. Is safe acceptable? Should you try your luck?

Whatever, you will have to swing harder, to try and force the ball out and the angle into the ball will need to be steeper to eliminate some of the thick

PRO TIP Having a few practice swings in similar grass length close by helps to gain a feel of how thick the grass is.

grass. This can be achieved by placing the ball position slightly further back in the stance. Finally, remember to hit the back of the ball – a common error is to get underneath it. On the fairway you may benefit from a little bounce on a fat shot, but not in the rough. The club will pass underneath the ball and flop forward just a short distance.

There is one other danger – a twisted clubface. This problem is dealt with on pages 204–205.

A "flying" lie

This is where the ball sits lightly in medium grass. Assess your lie carefully, but beware not to move the ball as you check it, or (as in the photo) when you address it.

Tiger Woods is good at every aspect of the game, but very good from the rough. Of course he doesn't get into trouble often, but his technique of strong wrists (see pages 204–205), a good eye, and clear focus help him play attacking shots from some very difficult positions.

Playing poorly from the rough
Altering your grip

There is one other problem with thick rough that may be easily solved. Sometimes you will find that your direction is all wrong – often hooked – because the clubface has twisted in your hands just before the strike of the ball.

Firm your grip

The solution is quite simple. Play the shot with firmer wrists. They need to be firm at impact but the key is to tighten the grip at the start of the swing. This extra gripping will translate from the hands to the wrists.

When keeping the wrists firmer you are likely to have a shorter follow-through. This is because the wrists are usually rotating with the momentum. A slowing of speed as the club hits the grass makes the club automatically finish round the player's back. It is the combination of firmer wrists and the thicker grass slowing the swing down that creates a shorter follow-through.

Improvise your shot

Don't worry about not playing a full elegant swing. A shorter jab will suffice, especially if the ball gets clear of the rough and ends up somewhere near your target area.

Lines and angles

Strong wrists and coming down from a steeper angle are crucial in this shot. Although the ball sits in a difficult lie (left) the player is lucky that it didn't roll a few more feet into trouble. If you get a let-off like this, make full use of it.

The same shot with the view of what lies ahead (right). The ideal line towards the pin is blocked by the bushes so the player has to play out onto the fairway. The high fencing ahead marks the edge of the practice ground on this course and out of bounds. A jabbed wedge will move the ball safely 90–100 yards up the fairway.

REMEMBER

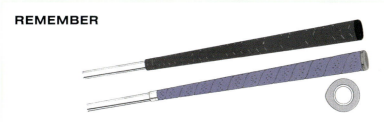

The actual grip on your shaft will make a difference to your game and your confidence. Try out grips and choose one that you feel most comfortable with. They are normally leather or compound, corded, or ridged. In the rough always use a glove, and make sure your glove and grip are dry. Firm up your grip for the shot from the rough. Note too that the shaft grip may be slightly ridged and not completely circular.

PRO TIP Don't be tempted to try to overhit as any slight misjudgment will be amplified in the rough.

Still scoring worse than you hoped Is your approach the right one?

Although many people talk about the physical side to golf, there is the mental side, too. There are numerous ways in which you can readjust your scores – and your attitude toward your scores.

Be realistic

The first "solution" might be to look realistically at your scores, hole by hole, round by round. We all expect to par every hole which of course is impossible. So analyse your score in relation to your handicap, remembering that you're not expected to hit your handicap every round, only when you're playing well. If this doesn't help, look at your score in relation to where it was one year ago. The chances are that it is better.

Build on the positive

If this fails to lift your spirits, remember the positive comments your opponents or partners made about your play last time out. There were some good shots, no doubt. If you are determinedly depressed about your golf score, then try some more practical suggestions on the course:

- remind yourself of the big picture – matchplay or strokeplay? This will mean you are making better decisions about shot choice;

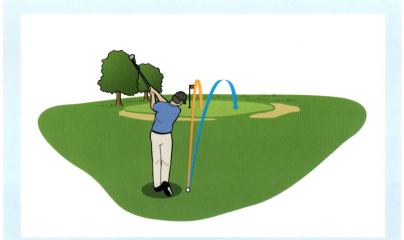

Be a winning player

There is no right answer to this fairly common scenario. The approach over the bunker may give you the better birdie or par chance, but it could also leave you in trouble. The apparently safer shot might not be well executed so you don't gain much advantage. The answer is that your approach should be determined by a range of factors largely decided on the day. The important thing is to make a fresh decision every time. Don't tell yourself you are simply an aggressive player and go for everything. Be a winning player, and make a good decision.

- what's your card or score like now – do you need to attack, how's your opponent doing? This will help you avoid reckless play; 18 holes is a lot;
- what hole are you playing – how many are left? Remind yourself of the time you last won three holes in a row or had back-to-back birdies. Things can turn around very quickly;
- what options do you have – is a once-in-a-lifetime shot even a remote possibility (probably not)? Don't go from bad to worse; try to get back to average golf, a platform on which to build.

This last point leads on to thinking about "percentage golf", which is not the same as course management (see pages 208–209).

The next shot

One good tip is to think about the shot after the one you are playing. What will you be left with if you hit your 3 iron? Could you hit a (safer) 5 iron and still have a good chance of reaching the green? Similarly, is there a nasty bunker between you and the pin? Would a safe shot to the heart of the green, taking out the bunker, leave you an easy two-putt? Is the high risk shot going to guarantee a one-putt?

PRO TIP Golf is a thinking game. Think about it.

Tiger Woods won the (British) Open Championship without using his driver, not because the course was short but because he and his advisors decided that hitting fairways, which Woods could do almost unfailingly with shorter clubs, was crucial. The rough was punitive. Hitting fairways not only makes shotmaking easier, but it also builds confidence.

Still scoring worse than you hoped Understanding course management

Course management is a department many golfers ignore or perhaps don't understand fully. Good course management saves you strokes. Course management is the reason top pros don't just stand on the tee and boom huge drives every single hole and why, sometimes, they lay up on par fives when they could get to the green in two. Attacking a golf course is fine, but sometimes a little defence is required.

Clear thinking

As elsewhere in golf, clear thinking and a back-to-basics approach may be all you need. When planning your round, you should consider several things, including conditions. If a course is very dry and fast-running then you may be more inclined to take out a club that will flight the ball lower and create more run – perhaps replacing a 5 wood with a 2 iron? Conversely, if a course is very wet

Distances in yards to green centre

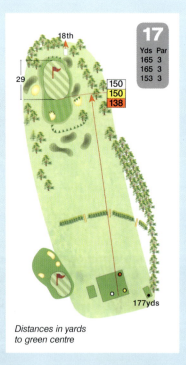

Distances in yards to green centre

Two pages from a course guide

Think carefully about total distance to a hole. For example, you may want to play 380 yards as a 4 iron and a 5 iron instead of a driver and 8 iron. The 437-yard par 4 shown here might be best played by most amateurs as three to the green. What three clubs would you choose to avoid the hazards?

then getting more carry on the ball will increase distance, so a hybrid or lofted wood may be favoured over long irons.

Club selection

There are times where the course may be extremely narrow and the best play may be to remove the driver totally from the bag. Course management is also about knowing your game in relation to the course. Think about course distances in relation to the club distances. Ideally go round the course before you play, noting the hazards and distances. A course planner booklet, sometimes called a "shot saver", can indeed be a shot saver.

You have the answers to the problems of course management, but you must be patient enough to apply them. Good course management will improve the score of a 12–20 handicapper by two or three shots per round.

PRO TIP Course management improves when you think about the course and not your opponent. Play your game and don't be put off by others.

Michelle Wie with her coach David Leadbetter (centre) and her caddie in practice for the US Open. Because most golf is played individually, we don't often get the advantage of advice from coaches or teammates. When playing socially it can be valuable to ask your partners what clubs they use or what approach they are considering.

Still scoring worse than you hoped Happy with your bag?

You and your clubs

A player struggles for all sorts of reasons and sometimes it can be a small, simple thing such as confidence. One important thing is to be happy – and therefore confident – with your bag. For example, keep old favourite clubs in the bag if you know you can return to these in times of trouble. With a maximum of 14 clubs you can normally afford to have one club in there just because you hit it well; it may not actually suit the course or the conditions, but it may get you back in winning form.

New clubs too can fill a player with new enthusiasm and focus, especially if they are custom fit. However, with new clubs remember to try them on the practice ground first. Similarly clean clubs can make a difference to your overall approach to the round you are about to play. The main point is to approach the round, and importantly the first tee, knowing what you have in your bag and how well you can use the clubs.

Balls, tees, gloves...

More than just clubs, however, ensure that you have everything else in order. Do you have enough of your favoured ball – marked with your initials or symbol – in your bag? Are you using the ball that both suits your game and the course you are about to play? Do you know exactly what kind of tee you use for each shot and have you got them in your bag?

Do you like water or food for a round? If so, take the extra minute or two to

Have tees that suit the shots you play. Know where your pitch mark repairer is (ideally in your pocket), and have your marker and pencil ready. These may be simple things, but it means one less item to think about on the course.

PRO TIP Hitting the ball well creates confidence so if you are striking the ball poorly, then get the shorter clubs out (they are easier to hit) and create a bit of confidence!

ensure that your bag has what you need. Do you know where everything is? It may seem petty, but being able to access your club cleaner or spare pencil without delay can keep you focused on your round and concentrating on the shot.

Nobody likes playing in the rain, but those who score best are those who have the waterproof kit ready to wear, have a good umbrella, and keep two or three dry gloves in the bag. Think ahead so there are the minimum of distractions.

You probably won't have the advantage of a caddie on a wet day, but do give yourself the edge by having a good umbrella, loose waterproofs, a good bag cover (to keep club grips dry), and several gloves.

Scoring better on the front nine
Consistency after a good start

Many players see golf as a game of two halves, but you should always think of it as just one round of 18 holes. Many players, however, do score better on the front nine, which can be put down to several potential reasons:

- although golf isn't the most **physical** of sports, it does involve a lot of walking and, if the average course is 4–5 miles long, then the first nine may take most of your energy.

A tired body can also create a tired mind and subsequent loss of concentration. You need energy for 18 holes, so if you struggle physically try using a buggy, cart, or trolley (or caddie!) rather than carrying. See what difference it makes;

- a key factor in golf is **concentration**, especially if a round is going to last four or even five hours. Unless you are exceptionally focused it

is extremely hard to keep your concentration all the way round. The tendency is for you to lose it in the back nine. A good technique is to only truly home in on your game when it is your shot. When you have down time then relax – switch off a bit. This doesn't mean you shouldn't watch other players' putts or note changing wind conditions, but do give yourself a break at times;

- related to both the above points is the issue of **warming up**. You will have been encouraged to warm up before a round and may have seen the pros spending a hour or more on the practice ground before playing, but beware. It is possible to overdo it so that, by the back nine, you are beginning to tire and have lost the freshness that is so vital. Make your warm up work for you.

PRO TIP You may be having a hot streak from, say, hole number 7. Keep this going as long as you can. Any break of concentration at the turn may be damaging.

Make your mind up what you are doing on the practice ground. Are you warming up or practising? Immediately before a round you should be warming up and reminding your body of the swing. Don't start trying new things just before you walk on course. Here Oliver Wilson of England warms up before the Pro-Am of the Estoril Open de Portugal at the Quinta da Marinha Golf Course.

Scoring better on the back nine
Building on your strengths

You will probably find, from your log pages, that you score better on the front nine, but this isn't true of all players. What if your back nines are consistently better than the front?

- The first likely factor is that you have played poorly on the front nine, feel out of the scoring, and are more **relaxed on the back nine**. The pressure has gone and suddenly you are playing well; there is less going on in your head. Now the player can relax. Of course the simple answer here is to play better on the front nine! The more practical advice is to try to learn the feeling of relaxation and enjoy the good shots so these can help build your confidence for the next round and, importantly, the next front nine.

- On pages 212–213 we talked about the dangers of overdoing the warm-up. Of course, the reverse is true and, without a warm-up, you may be very **slow to start**. In matchplay, and even more so in foursomes competitions, you might not have that many shots to play in the early holes; it may take you several holes to really get into your game. So, warm up sufficiently so that you have your eye in and your swing "warm". Only you know just how much, but very few players can play their best front nines when they have walked straight from the car park onto the first tee.

On pages 212–213 we talked about

REMEMBER

Try to keep your thoughts on an even keel. Excitement and anger (or frustration) can be equally dangerous to your performance. Try to keep your emotions on the same level throughout the 18 holes whether you are scoring birdie after birdie or racking up bogeys. Stay calm and focused. Take each hole as a fresh challenge, each shot as a new problem. Try the "Vardon" technique of obliterating everything but the target.

PRO TIP Always try to play your own game against the course and ignore the actions of partners and opponents – they will eventually disturb your concentration.

Any modern book on golf has to acknowledge the remarkable abilities of Tiger Woods. Commentators have analysed his many strengths and picked out his concentration as particularly important. None of us will match his swing, game-reading, consistency, or play from the rough, but we may be able to match his concentration. It would be good to have one aspect of our game comparable with the great man!

Losing confidence in your ability Getting back to basics

Golf is a game where form comes and goes very easily. So, accordingly, does confidence. The two are usually linked.

One key to working your way back to confident and good play is to understand where you went wrong in the first place. Were your problems fundamentally physical (bad swing, or poor technique), or mental (under pressure, or lack of concentration)?

Technical issues

If you have problems with the former then perhaps the best way of tackling them is to book a lesson. Your professional will be able to put you back into shape. A minor adjustment here or there may be all you need. Crucially you want him or her to strip away the bad technique and start you again on the right path. Without expert help there is a danger of building more faults, to compensate, on top of the fault you already have. It's not rocket science; the downward descent of your game (see illustration) needs to be broken, and a professional will help.

If you are unable to book a lesson then at least take yourself back to the default sequence outlined on pages 160–161. And swing slowly!

Sinking into further trouble
The downward spiral is quite common where one fault leads to another. Professional teaching or a radical re-start are the best remedies. Make sure you always keep your eye on the basic skills – don't try to over-complicate the game.

1 introduction of small error in technique

2 bad shots

3 adjustment to correct shot takes you away from good basic swing

professional intervention

4 more bad shots and other problems of technique

5 more adjustments

Back to basics

If your problems appear to be more mental than physical one answer may be to go back to basics. Remember why you play the game. You're probably not trying to win a Major, just trying to enjoy some exercise, meet with your friends, and hit some good shots. To achieve these simple goals you might as well be relaxed – tight muscles and a stressed mind do not lead to good golf.

Finally, on the mental side of your game, try to clear your mind of too much technique. Your body will have learned your swing. As you come to hit the ball you need to be thinking one thing only. It might be "slow" or "rhythm" or "follow-through", but don't overcrowd your mind with a whole sequence of thoughts. The aim is just to get the little white ball from one place to another. Keep it simple!

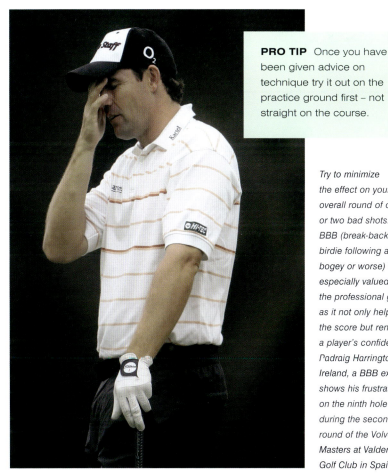

PRO TIP Once you have been given advice on technique try it out on the practice ground first – not straight on the course.

Try to minimize the effect on your overall round of one or two bad shots. A BBB (break-back-birdie following a bogey or worse) is especially valued in the professional game as it not only helps the score but renews a player's confidence. Padraig Harrington of Ireland, a BBB expert, shows his frustration on the ninth hole during the second round of the Volvo Masters at Valderrama Golf Club in Spain.

Competition and social play
Balancing your approach to improve them both

It's not the same every time you step onto the first tee. On some occasions you are playing for fun, with friends, and at other times you will be teeing up with strangers, maybe even with onlookers, about to take part in a serious competition.

You clearly don't have to have the same approach to both scenarios but you probably have the same goals –

to play well, hit some good shots, and improve your game in the long term.

Spot the trend
That's all very well, but many players (are you one of them?) play well in social games, but never seem to produce their best form in competitions. If you look at your logbook you may notice this trend.

Social play

1   Set personal goals for social play (such as a realistic number of pars or no three-putts). Your opponents do not know what your goals are.
2   Stay focused. Practise your powers of concentration in social

golf – follow the same routine for shots as if you were playing in a competition.
3   Keep a score in your logbook of every round – however informal it is. Learn from your mistakes.

Understanding your varying form

When playing for a score you probably take fewer risks. If a risky shot is attempted early on, and doesn't come off, then the chance of a good score has gone. Playing socially you may be tempted to be much more aggressive, often with good results. Learning to be aggressive at certain times can be vital because at some point aggression needs to be used during competition play.

Psychologically you are going to be more relaxed in social play, which, again, may lead to better shots. Of course, it might lead to lazy shots, too. The key to improving both social and competition play is to bring them closer together. Don't make them opposite ends of the spectrum.

Competition play

1 Remind yourself it is not the end of the world if you play badly. Everybody who plays knows that bad days happen.
2 Just swing slow and hit the ball – don't think anything different because it is a competition. Stick to routine and good practice.
3 Enjoy the fact that it is three to four hours away from work and the other stresses and strains of life.

Lacking consistency One step back and two steps on

Consistency is one of the words most used when talking to a golfer. If you looked at your logbook and checked your eclectic score (your best score on any hole on a particular course) you would probably be setting course records. The key question, of course, is why you're not hitting these good scores every time? Why are you so inconsistent?

Start with the swing

Consistency comes simply through the quality of strike. The first recommendation would always be to have lessons. Not only will you improve as a ball striker, but your understanding of the golf swing will also increase. You will know golfers who "have never had a lesson", but their play will always hit a buffer. You need to understand the swing to truly take your game forward and be really consistent.

Remember, however, that poor swings may have to be pulled apart before any positive changes can be made.

Practice and more practice

Once you have the swing under control, or at least on the right path, then practice is the key. Hitting more and more practice balls helps "groove" your swing. Grooving your swing basically makes it easier to repeat, and if you repeat your swing more often, then this automatically will improve your consistency level.

The important point here is to make your practice sessions count:
- identify targets on the practice ground and go for them;
- go through the correct preparation on every shot;
- use a variety of clubs (remember that short iron play is vital in good scoring);

- set yourself goals and scores – don't be satisfied with poor play just because it's not on the course;
- remember and build upon the positives – take the good shots onto the course.

Enjoy!

These last pages of the book actually take you back to the very first pages of the book. There are no magic formulae. The answer is to get good technique and practice. And to enjoy the game of golf.

There are no magic formulae to improve your scores, but many that you can work on. The result of improved technique will be better scoring and, almost certainly, greater satisfaction. Beyond that, one of the best tips that anyone can give is to remind all players that golf is just a game, played, as it always has been, for enjoyment. These gentlemen are Scots (who always play for enjoyment) playing at the spiritual home of golf, St. Andrews, in 1800.

PRO TIP The only real answer to improving consistency is to get a better method and practise hard.

Glossary

Address The golfer's position when preparing to hit the ball.

Approach putt A putt not aimed directly at the hole, or "laying up" close enough to make the next putt a certainty.

Approach shot One whose target is the green.

Backspin The spin on the ball applied by the loft on the clubface. A skilled player may apply extra backspin to stop the ball rolling forward on landing.

Backswing The first part of the swing, when the club is taken away from the ball to behind the shoulder.

Blaster Alternative name for the most lofted club, the sand wedge.

Borrow The slope of the green's surface; in response the player "borrows" to the left or right.

Bye Unofficial match played over the rest of the course when a matchplay competition has been won before the 18th hole has been played.

Casual water Water on the course that is not part of the design, such as rain puddles or over-irrigated areas. If a ball is in such water or, to play it, the player's feet would be, one can take a free drop. If there is casual water on the green, a ball on the green may be moved to the nearest place equally distant from the hole from which a putt will avoid water.

Centre-shaft Style of putter in which the shaft attaches to the middle of the head.

Chip A short running shot with a medium iron from just off the edge of the green.

Closed A relationship between the direction of the stance and the clubface. The clubface is "closed" or "shut" if it is angled towards the feet; the stance is "closed" if the front foot is across the target line.

Dead A ball so close to the hole that it can be assumed the next putt is unmissable; in matchplay that putt is conceded.

Dormie In matchplay, when a competitor leads by as many holes as there are left to play.

Downswing The part of the golf swing from the top of the backswing to striking the ball.

Draw A shot with a slight, controlled curve through the air, from right to left (right-handed players).

Drop When a ball must be lifted, under penalty or otherwise, the player, standing erect, holds the ball at arm's length and shoulder height and drops it not nearer the hole.

Eclectic A competition over several weeks or months, in which players record their best scores in every hole of the course.

Explosion shot The shot at a ball embedded in the sand of a bunker.

Face The surface of the clubhead that strikes the ball.

Face insert The extra hard impact area set into the face of a wood.

Fade A shot designed to curve slightly in the air, from left to right (right-handed player).

Fairway woods 2, 3 , 4, 5 (and sometimes higher-numbered) woods designed to be used when the ball is in play after the tee shot.

Flag competition Each competitor plays the number of shots derived from adding par for the course to their handicap. The player who gets the farthest (marking the place with a flag) is the winner.

Flange The broad sole of an iron club, particularly exaggerated on a sand wedge.

Flat swing One in which the club's motion around the body is low.

Follow-through The part of the swing beyond impact with the ball.

Fourball Match between four players usually two a side, using a ball each. The better score of each team at each hole counts.

Foursome Match between two pairs of players, each side playing one ball and taking alternate shots. Tee shots are taken alternately.

Fringe The collar of slightly longer grass around the close-mown putting surface of the green.

Grain The angle at which the grass of a green grows. Putting "against the grain" requires more effort than "with the grain".

Gross score The number of shots taken to complete the course before deduction of handicap to give the nett score.

Ground under repair Area of a course temporarily out of play, from which a ball may be removed for a drop without penalty; a ball outside the area may also be moved if the lie would cause the player to stand in it.

Half When opponents register the same score. A match is "halved" if it is completed all square.

Handicap Rating of a player's skill relative to par for the course. A 20-handicap player should complete a par 70 course in a score of 90. This stroke allowance permits players of unequal skill to compete on terms.

Hanging lie When the ball is on ground sloping down ahead of the player.

Hazard Any permanent obstacle on a course, such as a bunker or ditch.

Heel The part of the clubhead beneath the end of the shaft.

Hooded When the clubface is turned closed and inwards, reducing its loft.

Hook Faulty stroke when the ball curves to the left (for a right-handed player).

Hosel The extension to the clubhead into which the shaft fits.

Lateral water hazard A ditch, stream, or pond roughly parallel to the line of the hole. A ball picked out may be played from either side, with a one stroke penalty.

Lie The position in which the ball comes to rest; also, the angle between the clubhead and shaft that may vary to suit short and tall players.

Links A seaside golf course, typified by sand, turf, and coarse grass, of the kind where golf was first played.

Local rules Clarification of points about unusual features or obstacles on a course, itemised on the back of the scorecard.

Loft The angle on the clubhead to produce more or less height; also, to make the ball rise.

Loose impediments Twigs and leaves, not actually growing, and not adhering to the ball, which may be removed from around it without penalty. The ball must not be moved.

Lost ball If after five minutes searching a ball cannot be found, a competitor is penalised one stroke and plays another ball from the spot where the first one was hit, counting as third shot.

Matchplay Contest decided by the number of holes won rather than the total number of shots.

Medal play Strokeplay; contest decided by the lowest number of shots.

Nett score A player's score for a round after the handicap allowance has been deducted.

Open Of the clubhead, when it is turned out at the toe of the stance, when the line of the feet is to the left of the target (right-handed player).

Out of bounds Ground officially outside the playing area, marked by lines of posts or fences. A ball hit into it must be replayed from the original spot, and a penalty stroke is added.

Penalty In strokeplay, a rule infringement usually costs two strokes; in matchplay, the hole is generally lost.

Pitch shot A short shot to the green, hit high so that it will not roll on landing.

Provisional A ball played when it seems likely that the preceding shot is lost or out of bounds. It will count, plus a penalty stroke and the first stroke, if the original ball is not found; if it is, the provisional cannot be used.

Pull A straight shot to the left of the target (right-handed player).

Push A straight shot to the right of the target (right-handed player).

Rub of the green When a ball is stopped or deflected accidentally. It has to be played where it lies.

Sand wedge Iron, the most lofted club in the set, for playing bunker shots and pitches.

Scramble Team competition in which all players play from the site of their team's best drive, best second shot, and so on.

Scratch player One who is expected to play the course in par.

Shank Area of an iron's clubhead at the hosel; hence a shot hit by the clubface at this point, which flies off to the right (right-handed player).

Slice Faulty shot which curves left to right in the air (right-handed player).

Sole The underside of the clubhead.

Square The position of the body at the address when it is parallel to the line of the ball to the target.

Stableford A form of competition against par, using $\frac{7}{8}$ of handicap according to the stroke index. Nett par scores 2 points; one over, 1 point; a birdie, 3 points.

Standard Scratch Score The assessment of par for a course and the basis for handicapping.

Stroke and distance The penalty of one stroke and the return to the site of the shot before, when a ball is lost, out of bounds, or otherwise unplayable.

Stroke index The numbers on a scorecard indicating the order of the holes at which a handicap player receives strokes.

Strokeplay Competition decided by the number of shots taken.

Swingweight Measure of balance and overall weight of clubs. In a match set, all clubs should feel the same when swung.

Three off the tee If a ball is lost, out of bounds, or unplayable from the tee shot, the player is penalised one stroke and tees off again – the third shot.

Threesome A match in which one player competes against two, each side playing one ball.

Through the green The golf course, apart from teeing grounds, putting greens, hazards, and out-of-bounds.

Throughswing The part of the swing during which the ball is actually hit.

Toe The area of the clubhead farthest from the shaft.

Top To hit the ball above its centre; a topped shot does not rise off the ground.

Unplayable A player may choose to deem a ball unplayable, taking a penalty stroke and dropping the ball no nearer the hole. A ball that is unplayable in a bunker must be dropped in the bunker or stroke and distance taken.

Uphill tie When the ball is positioned on ground sloping up ahead of the player.

Upright swing Style in which the clubhead movement is almost vertical.

Waggle A player's loosening-up movements at address.

Wedge A club with an extremely lofted face: pitching and sand irons.

Whipping The closely bound binding at the head of a wooden club.

Wrist cock The natural hingeing of the wrist which begins as the club is lifted on the backswing.

Index and acknowledgments

Photos: p.1 Harry How/Staff/Getty Images; p.6 Aldo Torelli/Staff/Getty Images; p.7 TIMOTHY A. CLARY/AFP/Getty Images; p.8 Reeve Photography Marshall Editions; p.9 Reeve Photography Marshall Editions, r Reeve Photography Marshall Editions; p.14/15; Donald Miralle/Staff/Getty Images; p.16/129 Aldo Torelli/Staff/Getty Images; p.130/131 Reeve Photography Marshall Editions; p.132 Andrew Redington/Staff/Getty Images; p.133 ProTee United B.V. used with kind permission; p.134 Reeve Photography Marshall Editions; p.135 Scott Halleran/Staff/Getty Images; p.136/137 all Reeve Photography Marshall Editions; p.139 Reeve Photography Marshall Editions; p.141 Andrew Redington/Staff/Getty Images; p.144 Reeve Photography Marshall Editions; p.145 Richard Heathcote/Staff/Getty Images; p.147 Reeve Photography Marshall Editions; p.148/149 all Reeve Photography Marshall Editions; p.150/151 Jamie Squire/Staff/Getty Images; p.153 Harry How/Staff/Getty Images; p.154 Stuart Franklin/Staff/Getty Images; p.156/157 all Reeve Photography Marshall Editions; p.158 Reeve Photography Marshall Editions; p.159 David Cannon/Staff/Getty Images; p.163 Stuart Franklin/Staff/Getty Imges; p.166 all Reeve Photography Marshall Editions; p.167 Stanley Chou/Stringer/Getty Images; p.168/169 Reeve Photography Marshall Editions; p.170/171 all Reeve Photography Marshall Editions; p.172 Reeve Photography Marshall Editions; p.174 Goh Chai Hin/Staff/Getty Images; p.176 Reeve Photography Marshall Editions; p.177 Stephen Dunn/Staff/Getty Images; p.178/179 Reeve Photography Marshall Editions; p.183 Dean Mouhtaropoulos/Staff/Getty Images; p.185 Reeve Photography Marshall Editions; p.186 Scott Halleran/Staff/Getty Images; p.189 Stuart Franklin/Staff/Getty Images; p.191 Andrew Redington/Staff/Getty Images; p.193 Reeve Photography Marshall Editions; p.195 Reeve Photography Marshall Editions; p.197 Jeff Gross/Staff/Getty Images; p.198/199 all Reeve Photography Marshall Editions; p.201 Reeve Photography Marshall Editions; p.203 Scott Halleran/Staff/Getty Images; p.204/205 Reeve Photography Marshall Editions; p.207 Harry How/Staff/Getty Images; p208 Birdie Golf Ltd.; p.209 Travis Lindquist/Staff/Getty Images; p.210 Reeve Photography Marshall Editions; p.211 Timothy A. Clary/Staff/Getty Images; p.212/213 Stuart Franklin/Staff/Getty Images; p.215 Leo Mason/Corbis; p.217 Andrew Redington/Staff/Getty Images; p.218 Jim Cummins/Taxi/Getty Images; p.219 Scott Halleran/Staff/Getty Images; p.220/221 Bettmann/Corbis